POWERS THAT BE

POWERS THAT BE
(THE MAYFAIR LECTURES)

BY

ALEXANDER CANNON

K.C.A., M.D., PH.D., D.P.M., M.A., CH.B., F.R.G.S., F.R.S.M., F.R.S. TROP. M. & H.

MEMBER OF THE ROYAL MEDICO-PSYCHOLOGICAL ASSOCIATION OF GREAT
BRITAIN AND IRELAND
MEMBER OF THE BRITISH MEDICAL ASSOCIATION. (EXECUTIVE COUNCIL
1934-5)
MEMBER OF THE SOCIETY FOR PSYCHICAL RESEARCH, LONDON
MEMBER OF THE SOCIETY FOR THE STUDY OF INEBRIETY, LONDON
MEMBER OF THE SECTIONS OF PSYCHIATRY AND NEUROLOGY OF THE ROYAL
SOCIETY OF MEDICINE, LONDON
VICE-PRESIDENT OF THE UNIVERSITY OF HONG KONG MEDICAL SOCIETY
KUSHOG YOGI OF NORTHERN THIBET
MASTER THE FIFTH OF THE GREAT WHITE LODGE OF THE HIMALAYAS

AN EVEN DEEPER AND MORE AMAZING
STATEMENT AND ANALYSIS OF THE
MYSTERY AND POWER OF LIFE BY THE
AUTHOR OF THE INVISIBLE INFLUENCE

NEW YORK
E. P. DUTTON & CO., INC.

Eleventh Printing, February 1967

TO THE HIGHER

POWERS THAT BE

THIS BOOK IS DEDICATED

CONTENTS

PREFACE

I AM a man acquainted with miracles. The unusual, the supernatural, the transcendental, is not unusual with me. My recent popular writings bear eloquent testimony to *that* fact. Yet I confess that I was, and still remain, a little dumbfounded by the miracle of the public response to my popular book—THE INVISIBLE INFLUENCE. This response began almost at once to resemble a mountain-torrent: there was never much of the rivulet about it. It poured in from the North, from the South, from the East, and from the West: from Land's End to John o' Groats, and from the Atlantic Coast to the Isle of Thanet. It came to me clothed in the familiar envelope; it came by telegram, telephone—in short, it came by all possible means of communication, both time-honoured and modern. By the radio, the cable, the aeroplane, and the steamship, a foreign torrent lent its weight to the "home waters." It came from mechanistic and utilitarian (yet psychic) America, and from the dreaming deserts and mountains of the East alike. It came from business men and occultists, parsons and Indian colonels, doctors and judges, hard-headed lawyers, and women haunted by Poltergeists.

It was unbelievable and unprecedented in
its catholicity and its cosmopolitanism. It was
a miracle in itself.

It revealed to me what I could not have made
myself hope—that there is a growing army of
people, even in this materialistic Western
world, crying for the light. It shows me that
under the spurious trappings of this false
civilization there burns the ardour of men and
women who are alive to the existence of the
invisible world and its influence. It makes clear
to me that there is a longing for the day when
the great truths so long buried in the East shall
be revealed to all men.

Truly is this age an age of the outpouring
of the Spirit. Our young men are seeing visions,
and our old men are dreaming dreams, because,
as was foretold of old time, the Great Day of the
Lord is near at hand, and this civilization is
ready to give place to another that is nearer
shaped to the invisible Kingdom of Heaven.

These young men have written to me telling
me of their dreams : these old men have written
to tell me of their visions. And the wives of these
men, young and old, have borne them eloquent
testimony. The new age is being born; it is
coming ! it is here ! for it is ready shaped in its
eternal purity in the invisible Kingdom.

When the torrent of world-testimony came
pouring in upon me, I decided that I would
select the best letters and publish them under
the title of KARMA—because they are, indeed,

the KARMA, or Come-Back, of my outgiving
in THE INVISIBLE INFLUENCE.

But another activity came in front of that
intention: I received telepathic instructions
from the Greater World to go out and lecture
in such spare time as I could muster from my
medical and official duties.

I went to the most cosmopolitan centre I
could find, the West End of London, and there,
as well as in our great University of Oxford
and other Seats of Learning, I gave forth what I
knew in the simplest and most direct language
I could find. In those lectures I bore to the
West testimony of the greater knowledge of the
East, that he who has ears might hear.

I told my hearers of the *Powers That Be*—powers
which we, as sons of God, have latent in us.
I told them that we live in a world incom-
parably greater than anything imagined by
Western science. I told them of the wonders of
the East, and of the marvels of Eastern knowledge of the power of Mind over Matter.

With these lectures came a clamour for their
publication. "Let us read what you have said!"
my listeners pleaded, "for our minds cannot
retain so much that is novel and strange to us."

So, in response to their request, and because
the lectures are more intimate than the letters
and cannot therefore bear delay, I am sending
them forth in print—in a form as near to the
original lectures as is compatible with author-
ship.

A word concerning the lectures themselves!
There is one great truth which I have
endeavoured to make plain throughout, and
that is that Life is Eternal. There is no Death!
Man has latent powers of untold value within
his own mind. He has three bodies, a physical
or Earth body, an astral or Soul body, and an
etheric or Spiritual state.

Reincarnation has also been proved in my
last lecture by very forceful demonstrations.

I have endeavoured to make the reader think
aright and enable him to choose his designs
carefully before he paints them upon the canvas
of his mind. If only the reader will follow this
advice his mental pictures will be painted with
masterly strokes of power and decision; the
Thought will then become the Thing, and Life
will at last be understood by a world which
now is seething with unrest and seeking in vain
for peace. Herein is revealed the way to true
peace and happiness; to real power and to true
greatness.

If you were going abroad you would do
all you could to find out all about the places you
intended visiting and to see which hotels you
could stay at. But how much more important it
is that you should find out all you can about the
real life and next world. *You will all go to this
next world* sooner or later. To have no knowledge of this world is to be cast into the ' outer
darkness' referred to in the Bible where there is
undescribable sin, sorrow and suffering through

ignorance of the Powers That Be. Be thoroughly acquainted with your future spiritual journey, lest in an hour when you think not your earth-life be taken from you and you will know not what has happened or what to do. If you doubt these words of mine, I command you to read the Bible as it stands without any false man-made interpretation, and in so doing you will have your spiritual eyes opened and you will understand in the real and true sense God's laws and word. Read the truths contained herein and live no longer in a fool's paradise.

I wish to take this opportunity of thanking Mr. Francis J. Mott, the managing director of my Publishers, for the endless care and trouble he has taken in the preparation of this work.

My grateful thanks are due also to my old friend Dr. David MacLeod, now in the Greater World, for all the help and inspiration which he has never ceased to provide.

Peace be with you!

ORIENTAL HYPNOTISM
(The Secret of Mind-Power)

(Based upon a lecture given at various times and places, and more recently in a modified form at the Grotian Hall on 1st June, 1934.)

Oriental hypnotism is one of the secrets of the Yogis. Among other things, it enables etheric vibrations to be produced mentally and to be projected over a great distance. Such a projection of power will induce an hypnotic state in all who may enter that area. Incidentally, it is by this method that such phenomena as the much-discussed Indian Rope "Trick" are performed.

CHAPTER ONE

FROM time immemorial people of all nations have been seeking to understand the secret of the mastery of mind over matter. It has been the mystery of the ages; the Great Secret of all times; it has proved the *ignis fatuus* of the alchemist and of the modern scientist alike; but for thousands of years it has been known to the East, where it has been preserved in the silent monasteries of the Himalayas and in the snows of Northern Thibet. There, for untold centuries, the *Yogis* have been unravelling the secrets of the ages: there did we make pilgrimage, as I have already, in part, described in my book THE INVISIBLE INFLUENCE,* and there learned

* Published by Rider & Co., 34 Paternoster Row, E.C.4. (5s.).

something of the mysteries known to the *Yogis*.
To-day, I am prepared to enlighten you a little
as to the broad principles upon which the *Yogi*
bases his fabled control of what is wrongly
called matter; though I am not permitted to
reveal more than a tithe of what is known.

To begin with, let us glance very briefly over
the fundamental facts upon which the *Yoga*
philosophy is based. This is very necessary, for
no one can begin to think clearly about these
things unless, indeed, he has a "Chart of Life"
into which he can fit the new ideas which are
being offered to him.

You must try to understand the relation of
the world to its Creator, and to understand that
all that is real is of God. If you would find
true knowledge (*Knana Kanda*) you must be
prepared to surrender the belief that the
universe is built up of different substances, for
indeed such a belief is but one of the basic
illusions of the human mind from which all
other illusion springs. Having conquered that
belief, you will be ready and more able to
escape from the illusion of the senses which
underlies the material world.

Begin, my friends, by realizing clearly that
there is but One Substance: there is nothing
but the Universal Spirit, the *Paramatma* of the
Yogi, and that all things in the universe about
us are reflections of that One. Indeed, the
Universal Spirit may be likened to the sun,
and the world of matter and sense may be

likened to a vast collection of cups of water, each one giving forth a reflection of the one universal Sun. Every star, every flower, every man and woman, is but a reflection of this great Universal Spirit, and, therefore, no matter how diverse may seem the various manifestations of life, they are really one in origin. The Universal Spirit of Life remains one indivisible unity, and whatever was, is, or will be, whether formed or formless, exists in the Eternal Now of the Universal Spirit that knows no Time or Space.

The reflection of this One Spirit by the "innumerable cups of water," as we have called them for the sake of illustration, is called by the Hindoos *Mayâ*—the Great Illusion. By this term the Hindoos mean to indicate that the visible universe does not exist as an eternal verity in itself, but that it exists as a reflection of the eternal verity of God, and in this sense is clearly an illusion. *Mayâ* is the mother of the visible universe, and were that illusion destroyed, the world as we know it would certainly cease to exist.

It should not be thought, however, that we can treat the physical universe as being of no account because it is in the deepest sense an illusion. For it is a reflection of God, all that we can know of Him—and surely even the reflection of God is fit for the deepest worship and reverence! This illusion of reality, which we call the earth, manifests by reflection the law and order of the Universal Spirit, and the illusion is manifested in reflected accord with that unseen power. The emanation of the material world has proceeded forth in this order: first from the ether came the air; then from the air came fire; from the heart of the fire the waters issued; and from the bosom of the waters came the earth. From the earth arose the teeming life of the world, which, although it has many forms and many names, is one with the earth, and the fire, and the water, and the air—for they are all a reflection in the Ether of the one Universal Spirit.

Distinctions arise merely through names and words, but real differences do not exist: the great Almighty God who manifests them alone exists.

Do not underrate the importance of a true understanding of the picture I have painted for you: it is no use your setting out on a journey unless you believe that there exists a route that is able to be mapped out by you and to be traversed by you. Similarly, it is no good your setting out to try to produce the powers which the *Yoga* philosophy makes clear to you unless you understand the sort of universe in which you are really living. For, if you believe in matter as a solid reality, after the manner of the West, then you can never really have faith enough to perform the works that you otherwise would. For the faith cannot shake an enchained imagination, and the powers of the

Yogi could not work if the world were really
"a fortuitous concourse of atoms," or a "solid
structure" in which Mind was only a production of the brain, and dependent upon it
in the same way that a candle-flame is dependent upon the existence of the candle. You
must, as I have said, bring yourself to realize
that the world is the result of *Mayâ*, the great
illusion; for it will not insult your intelligence
to believe that an illusion is controllable by
those who can create illusion and can also
dispel it. Your imagination, thus released, will
be a tool to your faith.

You have to make your own personal escape
from the toils of this illusion—to get back to a
realization of yourself and your life as reflections of the one God. When you have got to the
point of such an escape you will find yourself
able to control illusion; to create it and to
destroy it again; to clothe your thoughts in
matter and to disintegrate the matter again.
This is the power of hypnotism as it is known
and practised in the East—for the power
which is practised in the West is not worthy
of the name.

To escape from the power of illusion and to
make yourself instead its master, you must free
yourself from the toils of bodily desire—yes, and
of spiritual wrong desires too, for the wickedness of the body is as child's play to the terror
of spiritual wickedness. Desire is the main-
spring of *Mayâ*, and you cannot hope to gain

control of the Great Illusion whilst you yourself remain in the grip of desire.

You must leave both the claims of virtue and of vice if you would engage in the pursuit of the true knowledge (*Knana Kanda*), and you must prepare your body by the means which I shall now expose to you whereby it can be purified and your spirit released from the chains of illusion.

Once that is achieved you may learn how to induce the *Samadhi* (the ecstatic trance); how to create insensibility in others; how to create illusions, and to practise the art of levitation. All these things may be done by the understanding and practice of *Yoga*, for by *Yoga* you may learn the secret powers of the Universe (the *Kechara*) and you may conquer all the spirits that move in the air. This power will come to you if you are pure in heart, free from vice and from desire, and if you will contemplate the reality of the Universal Spirit of which all life is but a reflection. No matter what your life may have been; if you begin *now* earnestly and utterly to renounce all those false values of pleasure and sin, virtue and vice, and become utterly blameless and pure in body and in motive you will be made utterly free from the power of sin. Some of the great saints of history did not begin too well in their recorded lives. It is not how you start but how you end that counts.

When you have conquered your desires and

thereby have gained in magnetism, you will be able to lay your hands upon the sick in such a way that they will recover. There is, in fact, no limit to the power which you may gain as you go on in the study of the methods and observances for generating your personal magnetism; but I cannot, in this all too brief lecture on this stupendous subject, dwell upon the details of such development; nor, indeed, would I be permitted to reveal them all to you.

One thing is certain, however, and that is the gain that must accrue to you in the shape of personal success and peace. For as soon as you have attained to control of your desires you will experience that *peace of God which passeth all understanding*,* and the forces amid which we all move so blindly (like bulls in a china-shop, as most of us do in the West) will be bent to aid us and to sweep us along to true success. It will be the measure of your faith in the unseen powers which you are harnessing that will determine your advance. If you are a disbeliever; if you have no faith; or if you are addicted to the pleasures of the senses, you can never achieve real success.

Now for some practical advice to you.

You have had the way briefly mapped out for you; you now understand the sort of universe in which you dwell; you know that it is not just a lump of solid matter floating in immeasurable space, but you realize instead

---

* Philippians 4 : 7.

that it is a reflection of the living Spirit. The country has been reconnoitred for you—it is time for the first steps of the march to begin.

You begin by gaining control of your lower forces through the Life Principle, or *Prana*, and by concentrating your mind. These processes run, as it were, in double harness, for in concentrating your consciousness upon the highest ideals, you are at the same time withdrawing your consciousness from the lower forces of desire. Remember that you must not try to catch up with the Orientals in this matter all at once. They have generations of this sort of thing behind them, and were conscious of this power when your forefathers were running about with painted bodies. In consequence of this, the Oriental has a more strongly developed will and, hence, more natural magnetism.

Purification and concentration are best obtained in peaceful and beautiful surroundings. If you would gain them for yourself, I command you to retire to some place where, surrounded by beauty, and peace, and by beautiful odours, you may get for yourself peace of mind and uninterrupted concentration. Here you should begin also the practice of breath control,*

---

* The relation of breath-control to thought is not at all realized in the West. Steady and deep breathing is intimately connected with steady and deep thinking.

The Western mind will not appreciate its importance until the chapter on telepathy in this present volume is assimilated.

I have shown in that chapter some results of the use of my psychograph which records the emotional reaction of a person's mental processes upon his breathing.

known to the East under the Sanscrit name of *Pranayama*. Sit on the floor with your legs crossed * and begin to practise that most valuable method of breathing known as the *One-Four-Two rhythm*.

This consists of inhaling through the left nostril for eight seconds, retaining the breath for thirty-two seconds, and then exhaling gently for sixteen seconds through the right nostril. The meaning of One-Four-Two is obvious to you as the relationship between the times of inhalation, retention, and exhalation of the breath. When you have completed the above ritual, you must then "change over" nostrils, as it were, and inhale for eight seconds through the *right* nostril, and, after holding the breath for thirty-two seconds as before, exhale through the *left* nostril over a period of sixteen seconds.

When you have completed the cycle in this way, you should begin again at the beginning by inhaling through the left nostril, and so on. As to the number of times this exercise should be repeated, and as to how often you should do the exercise, this is entirely a matter of individual discretion. The average man should proceed carefully, and remember that the more difficult stages of the *Yoga* philosophy require a proper teacher or *Guru*, as he is called. I am telling you only the beginnings of self-purification and of right desire, for it is a saying in the East that *When the "Chela" (the student of*

---

* In the Buddha attitude.

Yoga) is ready, then the "Guru" (the Teacher) appears. There is a subtle sympathetic telepathy between all men as soon as they free themselves from false desire and are purified. They get, as it were, on to the wave-length of the Great Ones and the *Guru* certainly appears. Have I not told you in my book, THE INVISIBLE INFLUENCE, how that the Great Lhama and his brethren knew of my visit to the Orient even before I had myself made up my mind to go there?

Now, having practised this One-Four-Two rhythm, you must practise the control of your breath. Needless to say, during all these exercises you must keep your heart on fire with faith in the principles you are following. To develop the control of your breath, you should close the right nostril (*Pingala*) with the right thumb, and inhale through the left nostril (*Ida*). Having inhaled deeply, you must then close both nostrils and retain the breath for as long as possible without strain. When you can hold the breath no longer without discomfort, breathe out slowly and evenly through the right nostril. Never leave the lungs empty for any length of time, but commence to breathe again, this time by closing the left nostril and inhaling through the right one. Again hold the breath for as long as is possible, and then, reversing the procedure, breathe out through the left nostril.

This temporary cessation of breathing is known as the *Kumbakas*, and you should practice

twenty such *Kumbakas* at four times of the day—
twenty at sunrise; twenty at midday; twenty
at sundown; and twenty at midnight. Let this
be done daily without neglect and without fear
or doubt. It will cleanse your body and
destroy its impurities. Your body will be quite
rejuvenated, and you will possess a sweet odour,
your skin will become pure, your appetite and
digestion good, and your voice, though
becoming altogether softer in its tone, will
carry to exceptional distances. Great courage
will be yours, and you will generate a mighty
enthusiasm and overwhelming strength. In the
state of mind that will be induced you will be
able to steer your way with ease across the
waters of sorrow, dreary doubt and hardship
which are all over the world. Your personal
magnetism will be so increased that men will
feel your power and will obey you in whatsoever
you command them. You will be free from
disease and pain, because you will be free from
the illusion of the world.

Of course, you will meet with many other
exercises as you advance in the study of the
Yoga philosophy, and each of them will increase
your magnetism and your freedom from
illusion. But the first step is this *Pranayama* of
which I have told you, for it is the beginning of
the mastery of your mind over matter. Once
again let me warn you not to try to overdo it at
first. Go carefully, for you have not the power
to vie with the Orientals in the speed of achieve-

ment. But for you, as for them, the beginnings
of power lie in the control of breath. It is by
these means that the Oriental comes to a point
where he can simulate death and be buried, as
indeed he is*; and it is by these means that the
Adept can eventually walk on the air, and
transport himself into other bodies. However,
you must remember also that the Great Ones
do not bother with such feats, but leave them
to the Fakirs.

After three months of careful practice of the
Pranayama you can begin your hypnotic tests.
Your subject should be nude, or at most be
covered with a thin garment. He should lie
on his back and place his arms lightly by his
side. There is no need for you to make him
gaze fixedly at a metal disc, or to wave your
hands in the air as the Western hypnotists do.
There is no need to say "Sleep!" to him or to
utter a word to him by way of command.
You simply fix your subject mentally at the
Glabella (between the eyes) and think of the
perfection of Life. Then you make yourself
light and pure by *Pranayama* and direct him to
concentrate his attention within his mind: tell
him that there is a hole in the very centre of his
brain, where grows the *Thousand Petalled Lotus*,
or *Gem*, as it is called in the East. Tell him to
imagine that he sees a light in this hole, and
bid him draw up his breath into that hole and
to think of nothing else but the filling of it

---

* See pages 147 to 150.

with his breath. Tell him that this *Thousand Petalled Lotus* is most glorious in radiant light and that he must so picture it as he fills the hole with his breath. (Incidentally, it is of interest to note that the Lotus is situated at the spot where the Western anatomist has located the *Pineal Gland*—the centre of dreams of the old scribes.) You use nothing but your will-power, for by the power of the will alone you may bring sleep upon the eyes of a multitude. Now you, being full of light and of radiant power, will begin to make the four passes that will complete the sleep. Press your hands lightly over the subject's forehead, then pass them down over his ears and the side of his neck, and slowly over his breasts. The second pass is made in exactly the same way, but it is continued below the breasts and finished off at the navel. The third pass is again a repetition of the second, but it is carried on past the navel and along the outside of the thighs to the knees. The fourth pass repeats the movement, but is continued down the inside of the legs, along the inner side of the calves, over the instep outwards, and out at the toes. In all these passes the hands must be moved very slowly and very lightly over the breasts, and must not be placed heavily on any part of the subject. As you make these passes you must with all your heart and mind Will that the patient should sleep.

Whilst you are making these four passes the

subject will be putting his breath and thought into that aforesaid imaginary hole in the head between the eyebrows, and by the time this fourth movement is complete he will be fast asleep.

When sleep ensues, you still do not speak to him, for how can a sleeping man hear? All you need to do is to desire with all the earnestness that you possess that he shall overcome any difficulty of which he wishes to be rid. I am assuming for the moment that he is sick or in some way in trouble and needs to be helped. Desire him to overcome his illness, or to carry out some request, or to improve some latent or feeble powers, but do not utter a word to him. Place your hands upon his head between his eyebrows and speak through your mind with your vibratory thoughts. Will him to become obedient to you and to do as you desire him.

Should he be a sick man, you can cure him by the mere breathing upon him of your breath —for you, being full of light and radiant power, have healing in your very breath. If your patient suffers from any bodily pain, such as chill, rheumatism, indigestion, urinary troubles, or the like, you need only to breathe upon the affected parts thrice with your hot breath. To do this you must hold your mouth close to the affected part and form in your mind a vivid picture of your patient being perfectly well, whereupon the physical result will be just as you have pictured it to be.

If, on the other hand, the illness of your patient is a congestion, such as a disease of the lungs (pneumonia included), or heart disease, then you must breathe upon the affected parts from afar, so that the breath, full of light and of magnetic power, is cold when it reaches the affected part. Do these things with a full realization in your mind of their complete efficacy and your patient will be immediately healed.

The secret of this power lies in the control of illusion which you have gained through a long and diligent practice of breath-control and by the mastery of your desires. Is it not clear that ill-health is simply the distortion of the Great Illusion into an inharmonious illusion of suffering? Having power to control both, you have the power to heal disease.

Great as that power is, however, it is but a tithe of the power that is waiting to be developed in you. I have told you that you shall be able to clothe your thoughts in matter and to control distant objects if only you will be faithful in this thing.

Here, then, is the way to progress yet another step in the control of illusion. Sit with crossed legs, and fix your eyes steadily upon the tip of your nose. With the chin elevated, press your tongue against the teeth and draw in your breath very slowly until the chest is full. Hold the chest so filled for as long as you can, and then let your breath out slowly in a steady stream. During this exercise you must keep your mind filled with the fullest sense of the power and perfection of the Heavenly Father, and allow none but the highest ideals to enter in. If you find you cannot concentrate easily at first, you should exercise your faculties in that direction by holding some simple object in your mind's eye. Concentrate upon a gem, or a flower, or anything that might please and interest you. Do not be content just to think about it, but picture it vividly in the mind until you can see it clearly. This will probably not prove to be very easy, and your difficulties will teach you how shallow and evanescent your ordinary thinking is. You will realize that your mind has been accustomed to flitting hither and thither like a humming-bird.

You must daily repeat this exercise of concentration until you can see without any obstruction or lapse the object upon which you are concentrating. Soon you will be able to see the object in your mind, no matter whether your eyes are closed or opened. Continue this exercise until you can hold any desired object in your mind's eye for fifteen minutes without permitting another thought of any kind whatsoever to enter in. Once you have achieved this power your thought will take objective form, so that a person standing by will be able to see the object produced by your mind in space as clearly as you yourself are doing. It is, in fact, by this method that the Fakirs create

illusions, and by it a man can create the form
of anything he desires. I may say that I, myself,
have had appear before me the materialization
of a friend who, at the time, was thousands of
miles away from me; yet I have shaken hands
with the materialization and conversed with
him and he with me. At the same time, I have
seen a friend of mine, a quite famous Doctor of
Medicine, also shake hands with a materialization which, in his case, handed him a keepsake
which he still possesses. There is here much
food for thought.

This power is the basis of all materializations and is the *modus operandi* of the much-
discussed Indian Rope "Trick" which I will
deal with in another lecture in these pages.
We in the Occident call this sort of manifestation hypnotism, and think we have dismissed
the subject to our satisfaction (just as a yokel
might dismiss a reflection of God's glory by
calling it "only a flower"), but there is more
in the world than mere names, and the fact
remains that the people who see the Indian
Rope "Trick," or any other of these phenomena, are not asleep but wide awake. I was
talking not many days ago to a simple shoemaker (but a great mind, nevertheless) who
discovered that he possessed natural powers in
this direction. He told me that he once stood at
the door of his shop and concentrated upon an
imaginary sovereign lying in the gutter, not
with the object of influencing all passers-by,

but with the object of picking out a "sensitive," with whom he could work. After a long period, during which many people passed by without any result, a girl suddenly bent down and tried to pick up the coin, whereupon the shoemaker walked over to her and touched her upon the shoulder. The power of a thought to materialize depends upon the intensity with which it is held.

This is not just a flight of the imagination as you will now begin to see. And I can assure you that when you have ridded yourself of desire and have gained control of your breath, you will be able to put a thousand people to sleep simply by the exercise of your will.

For the will, when held steadfastly to one idea, is potent to control this *Mayâ* which we call the world, and a man whose faith is but as a grain of mustard seed may truly move mountains. It was no mere mysterious promise which Jesus, the Great Master, made to His disciples when He made that statement, but a real and true fact which will alter our ideas of the world completely if only we understand its inner meaning.

This "moving of mountains" has been whittled down until it meant "mountains" of doubt and difficulty. Well, you will be able to move *them* too (in fact, they will move themselves), but the truth that you may move actual mountains can be demonstrated in degree by the practice of levitation. By this power you can raise a subject from the ground or bed and make him float through the air at your will.

To do this you must first of all put your subject to sleep by the method I have already described to you. When he is fast asleep, you must Will that his body shall become as light as the air, whereupon, after you have made the necessary passes, you will be able to draw his body up with your fingers until he is suspended in mid-air. This is no joke I am making to you, but a solemn fact of a science as far above the science of atoms and chemicals as a cloud is above the earth. A Wise One may accomplish this feat simply by the exercise of a will grown strong through meditation and control of breath.

I have not told you as yet how you may awaken your patient. This may be done very simply by your cold breath directed upon his forehead, or between the eyebrows. Or, again, you may restore him to waking consciousness by passing your hands upwards over his body, reversing the direction of the passes made to put him to sleep.

Now I am coming to the end of my talk with you, but the end is always a new beginning to those whose eyes are open to the Truth, and, indeed, the end of my talk is the beginning of new power for you if only you will grasp the meaning of what I have said. For you can rise above the world as you know it; you can dispel war and strife, and bring peace and joy; you can clear your mind, concentrate your will-power, clothe your thoughts with matter and disintegrate it again, and you can cause heavy objects to approach you from a distance without a touch of your hands. For, of a truth, you have but to place your thought upon an object and *Will* it to come to you, and, behold, it will slowly lift itself and approach you at your command.

I have spoken to you of but a few of the minor mysteries of the East, especially of Arabia, India, Egypt and Thibet, but what I have told you is only a fragment of the Truth that is known to the Wise Ones of the Earth.

HOW TO GET WHAT YOU WANT
(A Study of the Magic Laws of Nature)

(Based upon a lecture given in the Renton Terrace Hall, Leeds, on Sunday, 6th October, 1912; at the Mayfair Hotel Tea-Talk on March 25th, 1934, and also delivered to the Bridlington Literary and Debating Society, January 23rd, 1934. Several interesting appendices appear at the end of this lecture, concerned with the various manifestations of thought-power which attended the occasion of the Mayfair lecture.)

A right attitude of mind is the key to the secret of success. A wrong attitude of mind is the instrument of what is called "Black Magic," and will bring into our lives, and into the lives of our associates, the evil imaginings of which we are the guilty harbourers. As the previous lecture has made clear, the world of sense, and space, and time, is a world of reflection: we and all about us are but the reflections in space-time of the eternal verities of the Godhead. We are like so many little cups of water in which the universal sun of God's spiritual nature is reflected. If we keep these little cups of water clean and clear we shall reflect a pure picture of the universal Good. But if we let the "water" in our "cups" become tainted and impure, then the image of God is distorted and faint.

It is by right-thinking that we keep these little cups of water pure and clean. And if we keep a watchful eye upon our conscious minds (the surface of the water in our little cups) we shall be able to prevent evil shapes from alighting thereon and, by natural action, sinking into the depths of our "cups"—our subconscious and unconscious minds—therein to ruin our lives and stifle our spiritual natures.

CHAPTER TWO

*W*HATSOEVER *a man soweth, that shall he also reap.* So says the Bible in the seventh verse of the sixth chapter of the Book of Galatians. How many Christians believe that with all their heart and soul? The Christian West has always claimed the Bible to be full of Wisdom but it has never given the Bible real credit for being a book which can be relied upon and proven to the hilt as a scientific treatise. Some people have, of course, relied upon it; but usually they have based their reliance upon a form of sentimentalism which has not succeeded in convincing others of the real virtues of the great book. Perhaps there *is* a good deal in the Bible that is mere history, and perhaps some of it is *not* very pleasing history, but the fact remains that, underneath all this, and especially in the New Testament, there is a vast store of knowledge concerning the way in which life should be lived if a man or a woman is to get from life its true measure of satisfaction.

I claim it to be quite true that a man reaps whatsoever he sows, and that the passage in the Book of Proverbs which says *Keep thy heart with all diligence; for out of it are the issues of life,* *

* Proverbs 4 : 23.

reveals the Ancients as being in possession of the knowledge of the sowing and reaping processes of life, and of the well-springs of disaster and of well-being which are to be found in our hearts.

You will notice in the Bible, that whenever it wishes to tell you to *guard* your thoughts or to *express* your innermost thoughts, it never speaks of guarding your *mind*, or of "keeping your *mind*," or of looking carefully into your *mind*. No, it always speaks of guarding your *heart*, or of keeping your *heart*, or of looking carefully into it. Now, there is a reason for this: it is not just a vague substitution of words. It means that the Ancients knew quite well that the faculty we call the mind is really the conscious mind, whereas the instrument *they* called the heart really meant the unconscious mind—the depths of your nature in which the power of your being is generated. It is there, in those deep springs of your nature, that the good or evil impulses of your life are bred. You had control of them once, when they were just passing flashes in your conscious mind, but you let them go unchallenged and unchecked, and they sank down into the unconscious, there to breed as a seed breeds when it is sown into the dark ground.

That is what sowing implies. It means the sowing of thought-seed into your own unconscious mind, and also the sowing of that thought-seed into the unconscious mind of the world. The one sowing you can do with your mind, but the other needs deeds also; those actions which speak louder than words.

Let us look at this sowing and reaping process in all its many aspects, for so many people are ignorant of these simple rules of life, and they go through life spreading good and evil thoughts around quite indiscriminately, thereby bringing havoc upon themselves and upon others. They are, as it were, not trained to be human beings. Unlike most animals, they have the power of directed conscious thought, but they have never learned to control that great power. They are, to quote the Poet's words,

Like little wanton boys that swim on bladders
. . . far beyond their depth.

They do not know that a knowledge of spiritual law is necessary to success in life, and that this law must be obeyed before it will become a man's servant. Obedience precedes authority, and the law obeys man when he obeys the law. The laws of electricity must be obeyed before the power of electricity is at man's disposal. If man misunderstands or misapplies the laws of electricity, then disaster is inevitable. So it is with the laws of the Universal Mind!

Remember that you are as a little cell in a huge body. The life of the body of mankind affects you, just as much as your life affects the body of mankind in turn. If you are not functioning properly, then to that extent you are affecting all the others in that body. If the body is not functioning properly because of some other cell's misbehaviour, then you feel the result. Think of the Great War! Think of the millions of innocent men, women and children who were horribly killed just because a section of men did not control their greedy, vain and murderous thoughts. That will show you how swift is the visitation of Nemesis upon those who hold evil thoughts, and also upon those who stand by and do nothing to check their growth.

For the law of life is a law of giving and getting. It is a law of action and reaction, and this implies that whatsoever a man may send out in thought, word, or deed, will return to him again. If he gives, he will receive. If he loves, he will be loved. If he praises, he will be praised. If, on the contrary, he hates, then he will find hatred. If he is harsh with others, he will live in a world full of harshness. Of course, he may not see his good or his evil returning to him *at once*; and many people have lost faith and have given up the fight when success was very near, because they did not know the meaning of the Biblical truth which promises reward to him that *endureth to the end.**
Life is no game of chance as is so often believed. It is like a boomerang, rather, that comes back to the hand that flung it; or it may be likened to a hen that comes home to roost and trails her brood behind her.

---

* Matthew 10 : 22.

In the East this law is known as the law of *Karma* (meaning in the *Sanskrit* the law of "Come-back"). It is the law of the come-back or back-lash of your thoughts and deeds.

So many people still believe that they can separate thoughts, words, and deeds. How foolish is such a belief! To say one thing and to do another! To think one thing and to say the very opposite! How absurd, really! Did not Jesus, the great Nazarene Yogi, say: *Ye have heard that it was said by them of old time, Thou shalt not commit adultery: But I say unto you, That whosoever looketh on a woman to lust after her hath committed adultery with her already in his heart.**

In his heart. . . . Mark the words, and mark them well. Not just in his mind: not just a fleeting thought that could be forgotten, but a deep-seated and powerful thing that has its foul hand upon the control-lever of the body and can make it do things which would put to shame the apparent mastery of the mind.

A man accused of evil will sometimes admit his action, but excuse himself by saying: "I'm only following nature." This is no excuse at all, and it should be a punishable offence to leave the unconscious mind unguarded by the consciousness. Your unconscious mind must be watched and controlled by stopping evil thoughts in the conscious mind. Remember that it is not sufficient just to be good in a namby-pamby sort of way. Letting what is

_____
* Matthew 5 : 27-38.

seemingly well alone does not always pay by
any means. Your unconscious mind may not
have been filled with deliberately evil thoughts
by your conscious mind (you may be what is
called "pure"), but all the time you may have
been holding little nervous, fearful thoughts; or
little mean thoughts, which like so many seeds
dropping into the earth, have dropped into
your unconscious mind and have peopled it
with nervous, fearful and mean shapes.

I believe that if you do not run your own
unconscious mind yourself, somebody else will
run it for you. Hence the adage that the Devil
will find plenty of work for idle hands to do.
Such idleness can be a very real evil. We
often sympathize with a person whose whole
mentality has been eaten up with idleness when
really we ought to shake him hard to bring
him to a realization of his responsibility. This
applies always to fear. No one *ought* to hold a
fearful thought. It is not a matter for sympathy
but for a warning; not a matter for weakness
but for strength: for whereas we have been so
apt to regard fear as a negative thing, it is
actually a positive thing which creates the
object of its own emotion. Fear is as dangerous
as disease and ought to be fought with great
power.

Let me give you some instances of the
operation of fear in the mind and heart. Let
me prove to you that what you fear will sooner
or later materialize in your life. Then perhaps

you will appreciate the great truth that fear is not passive, it is dynamic.

I knew a lady who feared an extremely rare disease. So terrified was she that she was continually living in dread of this disease, and bought every book she could find which made any reference to it. She feared it so much that she came at last to be gripped by a morbid fascination for the very thing she feared. Her end was dramatic. The disease, rare as it was, invaded her body and killed her. She had done with that disease just what I counselled you to do in the last lecture with a stone or a gem—she had held it in mind so tenaciously, and had concentrated upon it so effectively, that it had clothed itself with *Akhasa*, and the *Akhasa* in this case was her own body. She had controlled the *Mayâ* of her own body until it had manifested the illusion of disease. She died the victim of her own imagination. Just as I told you in the last lecture how to make yourself light with *Pranayama*, and how to cure diseases by holding the perfect picture of your patient in your mind, so this pitiful story demonstrates the reverse action—that of inflicting a disease upon yourself by fear.

Let me tell you of another case in point.

A man I knew who was worth thousands of pounds, was always joking about "getting ready for the workhouse" as he called it. He lived to repent his tragic joke, for as the years passed by his money vanished and he became almost destitute. He had so impressed the idea of poverty upon his unconscious mind that the Thought became the Thing.

A lady I know of was asked by a friend of mine during an epidemic if she had had the 'flu. "Not yet!" replied the lady brightly, thus indicating that she was expecting the illness, and that she was thereby preparing the way for the very thing she wished to avoid. Fear is at the root of all illness, for it checks the currents of vitality at their source. It lowers the *Prana*. Imagine the effect upon the men in a submarine if their commander, after looking through his periscope, told them that the waters up above were thick with enemy destroyers, and that they were utterly surrounded by nets and mines. Would they not be paralysed? Would they not think it better to give up the ghost, knowing that they dare not move because their engines would be overheard, that they dare not rise because they would be smashed, and that they could not stay where they were because of the slow death by suffocation. Can you not imagine the paralysing effect upon all their activities? They would be unable to do anything, because to them there would be no sense in doing anything. Life would suddenly seem a futile wait for death. Can you not imagine that this is just how the organs of the body feel when the brain, the instrument of the mind, sends down to them a cold blast of fear. Your organs cannot see anything outside the body: they have to believe what you tell them you can see in the outside world. If you see fear and danger, then your organs, like the submarine crew, will get depressed, and they will tend to miss the very chances of protection that otherwise they would have had.

Our bodies, like men under authority, need cheer and comfort. They are alive, you know, and not just lumps of fleshy machinery. They are sensitive living nations—millions upon millions of little cells all acting in their little way as tiny reflections, in tiny cups of water, of the Universal Spirit which you in turn reflect.

Therefore, give them courage, and give them hope. Dispel fear from them and lift the cold fingers of its inhibition from off their delicate functions. How can you do this? Why, it is simple. You must first KNOW YOUR-SELF, as the Greek philosophers commanded. You need to know that there is a perfect picture of yourself somewhere in your mind. It is perfect because you are a reflection of God, and the divine nature never makes anything imperfect. You must diligently seek after this perfect pattern which is hidden deep in your nature, and once it is found you must strive to mould your conscious life to its pattern. Those who do this need have no fear, for there is nothing to fear. The further you go on, the more you find yourself wishing with all your heart to live the right sort of life, the more you will become sensitive to the still, small voice of conscience within your soul, "heart," or unconscious mind. You will not, as so many do, look upon this voice as a sort of alarum bell which only rings when you are doing wrong, as though the only job of a conscience is to prick its owner. Instead, you will look upon it as the inner compass which answers to the Poles of God. You will begin to see that in following its guidance you are developing your own inner urge, and are fulfilling the perfect pattern of yourself which is contained in your unconscious mind. You will realize that your conscience is the little "wireless receiver" by which you receive the telepathic message of hope from the great Universal Mind.

Let me now give you some examples of the power of courage and of true faith to develop the real God qualities which constitute the real man, and also of its power to change one's environment to keep in tune with the new realization.

Let me tell you first of all about the young man who came to me saying that all he possessed in the world were the forty shillings in his pocket, that he was far from home, and that he had no prospects in life. "What can *I* do to change my condition?" he asked plaintively.

"Bless those forty shillings in your pocket," I said. "By that means you will multiply them, just as our Lord Jesus multiplied the loaves and the fishes." I then explained to him that Christ taught us that *everyone* has the power to bless and to multiply, to heal and to prosper. The forty shillings having been duly blessed, the young man was instructed to listen for his inner voice to tell him what to do. I told him that this was the telepathic guidance of his unconscious mind by the great Universal Mind, and that it was his unerring guide. After a while the young man said, "I feel I should like to go home." Now, his home was far away from London in the heart of the country: the train fare would absorb nearly all of his forty shillings; and there was no money in his home, nor work in the neighbourhood. Reason would have counselled him to stay in London and to look for work. However, when he told me how he felt about things, I commanded him to obey his inner voice (the dictator of his unconscious mind) and go back to his home, and I told him, moreover, that he must tell himself night and morning that the great Universal Mind would lead him into the way of prosperity. I told him that he could assert his claim upon his birthright, and that he could by divine right draw his own unto himself with an irresistible force, for God intended him to have all those things that were necessary to the fulfilment of his destiny. With these words I sent him on his journey.

For some weeks I heard nothing from him. Then one day I heard to the effect that a stranger had come to his village, had taken a fancy to him, and had almost at once put him in the way of earning several hundreds of pounds.

Another similar case was that of a man who rang me up to tell me that he had been summoned to pay five hundred pounds. "I haven't five hundred pence," he moaned, "and there is no way of getting any money either." I replied that there was a supply for every demand, I gave thanks to God that this man should receive the five hundred pounds, and I told the man to keep an unwavering faith in God and His goodness. However, the day drew near for the payment of the debt and no money was forthcoming. In desperation he rang me up to tell me that he was still without anything. It happened to be New Year's Day. "Don't worry," I advised him. "Nobody is going to issue a summons on you to-day. Pull yourself together! Act the part of a rich man! Show that you really believe what you say! If you do you will receive the money by to-morrow." He then asked me to dine with him that evening to help him keep his spirits up. When we met at the Ritz, I said to him: "Now, remember, this is no time to economize. Order a fine dinner. Act as though you had already received more than your five hundred pounds. Remember what it says in the twenty-second verse of the second chapter of Saint Matthew: *Whatsoever ye shall ask in prayer, believing, ye shall receive*; and don't forget to pay special attention to the word BELIEVING in the middle of that sentence. It is the *faith* that counts. And you have just got to prove it to be true by acting as though the money were *already* yours."

The next afternoon my friend was due to appear in court. He telephoned me at midday. "The money hasn't come," he lamented. "Why worry?" was my reply. "God is never late. He will take care of you. Remember the words of Isaiah: *And it shall come to pass, that before they call, I will answer.**

Well, it appears that at two o'clock in the afternoon, just as he was preparing to leave for the court, a wealthy relative dropped in to see him, and, upon hearing that he was called to court, and eliciting his financial state, sat down there and then and wrote him a cheque *for* £50 *more than the amount claimed from him.*

I may say frankly that I was a little relieved myself when I heard the news, for the man's faith was so weak and vacillating that he had actually delayed the gift by wasting his energies in fear and in preparing to attend the court. People *will* not realize that as the money is first made apparent upon the invisible plane, they must not jeopardize its manifestation on the visible plane by refusing to recognize it on the invisible one.

If you ask for success and at the same time prepare for failure you will get the situation

---

* Isaiah 65 : 24.

you have envisaged. Remember that it is not so much *what* you ask for, as *how you prepare for its reception* that counts. For mere words do not constitute prayer. *It is as a man thinketh in his heart . . . not in his mind.*

In other words, your actions are the real prayer. This being so, you must, if you would pray in real faith, prepare to receive the thing asked for when there is not the slightest sign of it in sight. When the three kings were in the desert without water, they consulted Elisha the prophet, and he said to them: *Thus saith the Law:* (mistranslated in the English Bible as Thus saith the Lord) *Make this valley full of ditches. Ye shall not see wind, neither shall ye see rain; yet that valley shall be filled with water.* * They did so, you will remember, with the result that the rain came.

Apply this Law that Elisha demonstrated to your own life, and *according to your faith it shall be added unto you.* The thing cannot be done without a struggle. It is not going to be as easy as you might imagine. "*Just believe?*" you will say. "*How easy!*" Believe me, you are making a great mistake. It is easy to *say* that you believe, but it is another thing to have *real* faith, and believe with all your heart. All along at first you will encounter doubt: you will hear a voice saying, "Don't you believe it, old chap. *You* prepare for a rainy day. Take *my* advice and don't be a fool!" This is the voice of the

---

* 2 Kings 3 : 16-17.

Tempter, and you must answer it by saying, *Get thee behind me, Satan!* You must throw the thought out of your mind.

There isn't any big accomplishment in the world's history that was not brought to pass by courage allied to vision. There is hardly a victory that was not immediately preceded by a grim fear, for *the darkest hour precedes the dawn.* Just before the big achievement comes, things often look utterly hopeless, and apparent failure and discouragement appear in a formidable guise. But this, too, is a biblical truth. When the Children of Israel reached the Promised Land, they were afraid to go in, for they said, *And there we saw the giants... and we were in our own sight as grasshoppers.** Take particular notice that they said that they were *in their own sight* as grasshoppers. It was a question of self-imposed impotence. *They were impotent because they were afraid.* Everyone is impotent until he replaces his fears by faith: until he realizes that there is a spiritual law in his own make-up which will operate if he will put it in the way of operating. He who understands this law *rejoices whilst yet in captivity,* because he can see with his "inner eye" the glorious picture of the promised land. In this way the three kings rejoiced whilst yet in captivity to the drought of the desert, because Elisha showed them the promise of rain as the fulfilment of faith. In this way a man must always see the goal from

---

* Numbers 13 : 33.

the very beginning and hold to the vision with unswerving loyalty and faith. In this way he may *demand* the visible manifestation of that good thing which he has already received on the invisible plane.

Jesus Christ gave us a wonderful piece of advice in regard to this principle of life. He said to his disciples, *Say not ye, There are yet four months and then cometh harvest? behold, I say unto you, Lift up your eyes, and look on the fields; for they are white already to harvest.** Christ was not the sentimental figure that has been made of Him by the world's misunderstanding. His clear vision saw the so-called material world in a manner quite different from that in which we see it. He saw what we may call the fourth dimensional world, which Einstein has but inadequately described in mathematical form. Jesus saw things as they really are in the Universal Mind; perfect and complete.

Jesus was trying to show his disciples that God has already provided for man more than enough, but He always taught that this provision did not take shape in a man's experience until that man had taken the first step and thereby proved his sincerity. *Ask, and it shall be given you; seek, and ye shall find; knock, and it shall be opened unto you.*† The promise of the great Nazarene was explicit enough. True prayer consists of putting yourself into tune with the Universal Mind: for whereas so many

---

* John 4 : 35.   † Matthew 7 : 7.

people think that prayer is the art of getting God to *give* something, it is actually the art of getting yourself ready to *receive* something.

It is your own insufficiency that stands between you and your ideals and your heart's desire. It is your fear that blocks the way. Jesus said, *Why are ye fearful, O ye of little faith?** and was always more ready to blame His disciples for their insufficiency when they failed to heal or to cast out devils (as healing the insane was called) than He was given to sympathizing with them for any helplessness.

When you can wish without worrying, every desire of your heart will be immediately fulfilled—though here let me warn you that I have more to say on this subject before I close, for do not make the mistake of supposing that you can just demand and receive, to consume the gift upon your lusts; for Jesus pointed out that abuse of the law led to failure.

In the Yoga philosophy we have a great saying: you will read it on page 153 of my book THE INVISIBLE INFLUENCE†—the book which will change your whole attitude towards life. Let me quote to you a few words of what the Great Lhama said to me as I passed from his presence. *Fear not any man,* he said in a slow but forceful undertone. *Fear not thineself; remember that fear is failure and the forerunner of*

---

* Matthew 8 : 26.
† Published by Rider & Co., London, 5s. net.

failure. Be thou therefore without fear, for in the heart of the coward virtue abideth not.

At the present time we are nearly all of us slaves to fear. But the day will dawn, and that day is not far distant, when men will realize that they are in themselves the generators of good and evil, and that the evil they fear is born by them of that fear. Then man will consciously take hold upon his own destiny. He will see that he is indeed the master of his fate and the captain of his soul. His release from bondage will come in a flash. The present earth will then truly pass away and each one, individually and collectively, will find himself to be living in a new heaven and a new earth.

And I saw a new heaven and a new earth . . . and there shall be no more death, neither sorrow, nor crying, neither shall there be any more pain: for the former things are passed away. * This vision foresaw the domination of mind over matter, the secret of which the Aryan Hindoos have known for more than three thousand years.

There is nothing new about this idea of the universe. The law of God has been the same and will remain the same for all time and eternity. There never has existed in the Universal Mind any death, sorrow, suffering, weeping, anguish or pain. These things are due to the fact that our "little cups of water," in which we reflect God, are muddy and impure

---

* Revelation 21 : 4.

through the admixture of fear and our own limitations. It is up to us to understand what we mean by that reflection and to clear our own instruments of their impurity. To do this we must stand guard at the gates of our own thoughts so that nothing in the way of evil or negative thoughts shall sink down into our unconscious mind. If they are allowed to do so they will breed, and breed, and attract other like forces to them. Did not Paul say, *We wrestle not against flesh and blood, but against principalities, against powers, against the rulers of the darkness of this world.** Birds of a feather flock together! Like attracts like! If your thoughts are evil or fearful you are hanging out a sign in the Invisible World that will attract the evil powers just as surely as the vultures are attracted to the carrion. Everything in the universe consists of vibrations. Your thoughts are vibrations, and they will not be picked up by those persons and powers whose "wavelength" is not yours. Think evil and you will attract evil people. Think good and you will attract good people.

I realize that I am using the terms Conscious mind, Subconscious mind, and Unconscious mind pretty freely, and I am beginning to wonder whether you understand exactly how I am using them. Let me describe briefly to you what I mean by these different "levels" of thought. Let us take an example of their

---

* Ephesians 6 : 12.

functions to illustrate what they are. I look
at the clock and observe that it is five o'clock:
my *conscious mind* has made an observation.
The thought is not lost, but it passes into my
subconscious mind and there it finds an answering
echo from a conscious thought I had made the
day before when I told my colleague to meet
me at five-thirty. (The contents of my subconscious mind can be recalled by a slight association but not so with the unconscious mind.)
This reawakening of an echo I call "remembering," and yet I find that, even though I may
have forgotten all about the appointment with
my colleague in twenty, thirty, forty or more
years ahead, I can, by being deeply hypnotized,
be made to remember every incident of my
life—even to such a detail as looking at the
clock and remembering my rendezvous with
a colleague, although it has now sunk down
into the depths of my unconscious mind. The
unconscious mind keeps within its depths the
secrets I have long forgotten, and perhaps it
even holds the secret of life itself. It is like
a delicate gramophone record of incredible
capacity: every fleeting thought is registered by
it, and in its depths, by the subtle connection
between it and the Universal Mind, each
thought re-echoes upon the very walls of Time
into Eternity. Realize this! Think what it
means! Your thoughts are your constant
prayer to, or your constant rejection of, God.
You are building up a great library of your

own deeds—a great autobiography which no amount of lies can ever hide from you at last. This is the record, the Silent Listener, which every man bears in his bosom, and this is the basis of the old stories about the Recording Angel, and his Golden Pen, and his Doomsday Book. Of a truth this is no exaggeration—no fairy story: the Creator knows the fall of every sparrow through the Universal Mind: do you suppose that your smallest thought is missed? No! It is penned against you, and though you may hide your thoughts from the world, the unseen law of Karma will weigh its forces for or against you in the end, and you will receive the blessing of God, or know the full horror of separation from Him—separation by your own hand from the very source of your being.

Now, if your unuttered and unmanifested thought can have such tremendous effects, does it not follow that your uttered thought will be doubly powerful? In the twenty-first verse of the eighteenth chapter of Proverbs we read, *Death and life are in the power of the tongue.* Just remember this fact and be doubly careful of the words you use, for how many a man has ruined his whole life by an idle word? The whole force of your desire becomes immeasurably heightened when you not only utter your desire, but when you also obtain the agreement of another person. Jesus, the great Nazarene Yogi, knew this to be true, for He said: *If two of you shall agree on earth as touching any thing that*

*they shall ask, it shall be done for them of my Father
which is in heaven** This being true, you should
not only trust in God, the Giver, and also the
Gift, but you should also trust in yourself, the
asker, and the recipient, and in other men who
must in the end support you in your right
desire. Yes! All men must in the end support
you if your desire be right and true, for in
the Bible we read: *Surely the wrath of man shall
praise thee: the remainder of wrath shalt thou
restrain.†*

Testimony is paid to the power of thought
even by those childish people who put their
faith in horseshoes and such talismen. For it is
their faith, pinned to the symbol, which gives
the horseshoe power to those who believe in it.
As an illustration of this let us look back a few
years to the time when our grandfathers were
much intrigued by the magic rods which a
certain American gentleman brought to this
country and sold by the hundred at a fat price
per pair. These rods were guaranteed to cure
all ills, and so well did they do their task that
their manufacturer and purveyor became
extremely wealthy, and was, moreover, lauded
in Pulpit and Press as a public benefactor. This
went on until a little group of doctors made up
a few sets of these rods from common everyday
materials, and, passing them off as genuine,
yet obtained exactly the same cures. With
this evidence they stopped the sale of the rods

---

* Matthew 18 : 19.   † Psalms 76 : 10.

and sent the American back home (with a fortune), and completely broke the "healing power" of the rods. Does this not prove the power of thought and faith to attach themselves to ordinary material objects? Does it not explain the mysterious power of shrines and ikons the world over? Moreover, is it not strange that people, having had such a convincing demonstration of the power of thought, should go back to their ills and their fears? Saying of the rods, " It was *only* faith after all." ONLY FAITH! One might as well dismiss a thunderstorm as of no importance by calling it *only a discharge of electricity!*

Only faith! Faith is everything in your life! *Eliminate faith from life and what remains?* Little or nothing that matters! *Keep* your faith, and the substance of your faith will come to you, for faith *is* the substance of things hoped for. Cast off fear and begin to live as though you knew the truth of this! Go on with the task of putting yourself in order first, knowing that the things needed to manifest perfection in this world are ready and waiting for you in the unseen world. These things will come to you if you act in the way to prepare for them. *In due season we shall reap, if we faint not.** Keep up the chin! Keep the flame of faith alive! Paint your house and keep it in good repair as though you were of some account, and the needs you have demonstrated *will* be met!

* Galatians 6 : 9.

Don't run away with the false impression that this is some silly make-believe, and that all you have to do to get a motor-car, for example, is to rent a garage. There must be some real need and some real meaning to your desire, and a real faith in your need and your God. Yet even what you may call "make-believe" will impress the unconscious mind in a most telling way. I know of a girl whose mother was at her wits' end because, although they were very poor, the girl was always talking and thinking of rings and things. *She never envied others*, but she lived in a world of wonders, and riches seemed real to her. One day, quite out of the blue, a wealthy man walked into the shop where she was employed and fell in love with her. Later she married him and her dreams came true. You may call that a child's outlook on life, but don't forget that Jesus Christ said: *Whosoever shall not receive the kingdom of God as a little child, he shall not enter therein.* *

Therefore, I say to you: Dream of a great future and that future will come to you! For *All things are possible to him that believeth.*† Fear will vanish when you walk up to it and face it like a man. The lion takes its fierceness from your fear: walk up to him and he will run from you; run away from him and he will run *after* you. Banish fear and you also banish evil. Love one another and hate will be no more.

---

* Mark 10 : 15.   † Mark 9 : 23.

Face a situation fearlessly and there is no situation to be faced. We often hear people talking about getting people to "pull the strings for them," but we may indeed wonder why they need to enlist such comparatively puerile help when, all around, never sleeping, never failing, there is this great Invisible Influence "pulling the strings" in the unseen world—those delicate, cosmic springs of life. Every word and every thought is an unseen vibratory "string" which "pulls" forces into operation in the unseen world. Think health, good, wealth, and happiness, and these things will come to you without getting anyone to "pull strings" for you. Think sickness, evil, poverty, and despair, and you will get them, even though all the King's horses and all the King's men are busy "pulling strings" for you.

Never despise the day of small things! Don't be a spiritual snob! Cast your whole energy into loving the little things as well as the big ones, for the little things presage greater ones ahead. You will get little signs of the Promised Land long before you see it. Before Christopher Columbus reached the great continent of America, he saw birds in the air, and twigs in the water which told him that his great day was near. So it is with your life!

The law of *Karma* applies with equal force to the lives of nations. Sometimes it takes time to act, but it never fails to do so. Take the

case of America and France. During the War
of Independence, France sent help to America;
La Fayette and his friends sailed to the help
of the struggling colonists. Over one hundred
years rolled by, and there came a day when the
Great War had been raging for four terrible
years, and the Allies were on their last beam—
to be candid, we thought we had lost the war.
We who were out in France were wondering
how to get the troops out of the Continent with
the least possible loss of life, for we saw that our
only hope would bè to rely upon the British
Navy. In London the news was received by a
thoroughly "blue" parliament. The message
had also gone across the seas to America; but
another message had gone with it on the unseen
wires of *Karma*; the reminder of the unpaid
debt of honour which America owed to France.
In the Capitol at Washington, D.C., amid a
silence whose depth it is beyond my words to
convey, the late President Woodrow Wilson rose
to his feet and read the message to Congress:
"Send us plenty of men and munitions and we
shall win." The hand of fate was over the vast
continent of America. The "strings" had been
"pulled" on the unseen plane: La Fayette and
his brothers reached ghostly hands back over
the century agone and signed the American
declaration of War on Germany. And so
America sent help to France. The law may take
a long time to operate, but what is put into the
world will again come out of it.

And now it is time to tell you of another law whose operation is bound up with that of the law of *Karma*: this is called the Law of Substitution. It is the law which assures that what you get is not what you want but what you deserve. Jesus plainly said that a man sometimes does not get what he wants because he asks amiss so that he may consume it upon his lusts. Imagine what a ghastly holocaust there would be if the thing were as simple as all that: if every thing that was wanted, even though it were not definitely evil, came in the way in which it was demanded. No, it is not the mere word of prayer that connects you with the Great Giver; it is your unwritten thoughts and your carefully recorded worth.

Many a young man has found himself in love, and has wished for the consummation of his heart's desire, but somehow there has always been some difficulty in the way. I am often asked to help people in love (yes, I get quite a lot of letters to that effect), but all I would ever consent to do would be to help you to get into that relation with the Universal Mind which will impel you to marry the right person. I would not take upon myself the responsibility of deciding what was right for you. Maybe you will find, if you do as I say, that the object of your affections does not come up to your expectations after all. You begin to question whether you have experienced a divine selection, after all. Later on you meet someone else who proves to be your absolute ideal, and then you say it is uncanny. I say it is not in the least uncanny—you are experiencing the operation of the law of Substitution.

If you had fought and scrambled to bolster up the false situation with the first person, you would never have found the real one; and this is why masterly inactivity is sometimes the way to success. There is such a thing as the law of non-resistance. *"Resist not evil,"* * we are told: *"Be not overcome of evil, but overcome evil with good."* † Resistance is hell, for it places a man in a state of torment. The Chinese tell you that water is the most powerful element in the world because it is absolutely non-resistant. It will find a way in where more direct forces would be powerless. It gives way before pressure, but in the end it will affect the thing that presses it. Dropping water wears away a rock.

These are great magic laws of which I have told you. The law of opulence, of substitution of health, of non-resistance—*Karma* with intuition and divine guidance. But there is a greater law than all these, and in which they are all contained. This law is the Law of Love. *In all thy ways acknowledge Him, and He shall direct thy paths.* ‡ In business, in pleasure, in every walk of life, however high or however low, we can never get away from the truth of the Gospel of Jesus Christ. For that gospel is one of

---

* Matthew 5 : 39.   † Romans 12 : 21.   ‡ Proverbs 3 : 6.

supreme love. It does not permit the entrance of any selfish thing. It does not permit a mere selfish getting, but balances a just account of giving and receiving.

A relative of mine used to say, *We gather whilst they scatter.* But what a misunderstanding this is of the great Law of Life; for this is not an interpretation of brotherhood, it is merely a selfish doctrine presented in Biblical terms. For there is a direct counter to such a false presentation of the Law of Life which says, *There is that scattereth, and yet increaseth; and there is that withholdeth more than is meet, but it tendeth to poverty.* *

This last is the law of a generous God for all men of generous minds, and it is clearly laid down in that greatest of all law-books; which is also a great scientific text-book, and a great story-book too.

You know well enough the book to which I refer. It is THE HOLY BIBLE, and I cannot do better than to close this talk with a passage from its pages which is indeed the keynote of my subject: *Seek ye* FIRST *the kingdom of God, and his righteousness, and all these things* (health, wealth and happiness) *shall be added unto you.* †

---

* Proverbs 11 : 24.   † Matthew 6 : 33.

APPENDIX A.

During the course of this lecture at the Mayfair Hotel, the announcement was made that a Medium to whom I had only recently been introduced, would take the platform and would go under control at 5.30, and the lecture would thereupon have to be abandoned for a short while to allow the public to see the Medium at work.

The Medium, a young man from Chiswick, a stoker by trade, then ascended the platform accompanied by a friend who had sponsored him. This friend, who had been a violinist, had lost the power of her arms and hands, but, by the treatment received through the Medium from a doctor alleged to be still living in Thibet, was gradually regaining the use of her arms.

The Medium sat on a vacant chair beside his friend, and the author went on with his lecture. Within one minute of 5.30 the Medium suddenly went under control, and began to speak English with an Eastern accent, assuming a mien quite out of keeping with his usual retiring disposition. Addressing the woman by his side as "Nurse," he began in a most imperious manner to order her to bring "patient number one" for his treatment. This she did (the patient being herself), whereupon he seized her arm in a most professional manner and began to perform a most able feat of manipulative surgery. Several doctors were on the platform, and they were amazed by the skill manifested by the Medium.

During this demonstration a most amazing occurrence took place in the audience. At a table near the platform sat a party of friends, including among their number Mr. Frank Leah, the well-known Artist and Sensitive. This latter gentleman was seen to be in great pain, holding his arms and making every attempt to massage his wrists. Eventually he had to retire until the performance was over. Questioned after this event, Mr. Leah stated that he could feel the mental radiations of disease which lay at the back of the woman's physical condition. Although this was unknown to the audience, it would, had it been known, have added considerable evidential weight to my insistence upon the wholly mental nature of disease.

After finishing his demonstration of manipulative surgery, the Medium then was questioned by me. I asked him very deliberate questions in a loud voice so that the whole room could hear, and also repeated the Medium's replies in a like manner.

The Medium answered the questions in an imperious voice and became annoyed by my insistence on behalf of the audience. "Can't you understand, confound you!" he broke out angrily upon several occasions.

The most interesting information given by the Medium was to the effect that Sound, Light, and Perfume were all curative agents in the order of importance given, and that the co-incidence of the three vibratory media could be effected with very beneficial results. He also told me that march tunes are the best for calming distraught minds.

In reply to the question Where do you get this information? the Medium replied testily, "Confound you, I get it from my great Master, Pythagorus, who taught all there is to know about vibrations."

The information was scanty owing to frequent interruptions, and by the fact that the Medium went out of control shortly after I had begun to ply him with deliberate questions.

I have since seen the same Medium under control of an entity who claimed to be the Master of the White Lodge. Strangely and interestingly enough, when so controlled the Medium always gives the true Yogi sign.

APPENDIX B.

After the lecture, a demonstration of the principles upon which levitation is based was given. Miss Kyra Nijinski, daughter of the famous dancer, was the subject, and although levitation did not actually take place, the body of the girl became raised to a pitch quite unattainable by any gymnastic means. Certain sections of the Press reported unfavourably on the incident, but the following resumé was afterwards made of opinions which came into my hands or into the hands of my publishers.

COMMENTS ON THE LEVITATION DEMONSTRATION

Dr. John Cunningham Duncanson, of the Ministry of Health and late Medical Adviser to the Borough Council of Woolwich, states that he saw the demonstration of the principles of levitation at the Mayfair Hotel Tea-Talk on March 25th by Dr. Alexander Cannon. He says: "The result was to my mind most impressive and I entirely disagree with the remark in the Press of the 26th March that all that was achieved was a difficult gymnastic feat. I am myself an old gymnastic champion and a medical man."

Dr. Thos. Mather Thomson, the radiation scientist and late professor (assistant) in Dublin, states that he is prepared to vouch for the fact that the subject at one point not only raised her head and chest from the ground, but also her hips by two inches, and, in fact, was commencing to levitate.

Mrs. Marie Freeman, the psychist of Knightsbridge, states that Dr. Alexander Cannon handed over to her for psychic training Miss Kyra Nijinski, the daughter of the famous dancer, who performed the feat on March the 25th at the Mayfair Hotel and that she has been actually levitated to the ceiling by the use of certain body vibrations used in the trance state.

Dr. Nandor Fordor lectured on "The Problem of Human Levitation" at the British College of Psychic Science on May the 31st, 1933, giving very convincing proof of the existence of this great feat defying all the known laws of Gravity. His lecture is published in the April number of the Quarterly Transactions of the College this year. Amongst the people who have been levitated are: St. Dunstan; St. Dominic; St. Francis of Assisi; St. Thomas Aquinas; St. Edmund, Archbishop of Canterbury; Blessed James of Illyria; Savonarola; St. Ignatius Loyola; St. Phillip Neri; St. Peter of Alcantara; St. Joseph of

*Copertino; St. Alphonso Liguori; Gegenwart of Vienna; Abbé
Petit; Henry Jones; Patrick Sandilands; Mary London; The
Drummer of Tedworth; Nancy Wesley (during John Wesley's
troubles at Epworth Vicarage); Harry Phelps; Henry Gordon;
D. D. Home; Victoria Claire of Coux; Mrs. Volckman
Zucarini; M. C., the sculptor; Robert Bell; Cecil Husk;
Eglinton (in the presence of the Emperor and the Empress of
Russia, the Grand Duke of Oldenburg and the Grand Duke
Vladimir); Ruggieri; Ira, William and Elizabeth Davenport;
Maria Vollhardt; Willy Schneider; Carlos Mirabelli; Covindas-
samy; Dr. Cannon and others.*

APPENDIX C

During the writing of this volume there came into my
hands a copy of THE NEWS CHRONICLE dated July 3rd,
1934, in which was printed an article by Mr. Hugh
Redwood, entitled DO YOU BELIEVE IN PRAYER.

Mr. Redwood reproduces there some of the letters
which have come to him, and by the courtesy of the
Editor of THE NEWS CHRONICLE I am enabled again to
reproduce them for your benefit. True, they are not more
spectacular than some of the instances quoted by myself,
but there is always an added interest in a testimony when
other, and disinterested, testimony is conjoined.

Mr. Redwood tells how The Missionary Training
Colony, Highfield Hill, Upper Norwood, had £8 of
bills to meet and nothing in hand to meet them with.
The men who ran it were convinced that God would aid
them, and they would, therefore, neither run into debt
nor issue a public appeal. Instead of this it cancelled
its standing orders with the local tradespeople and
waited. Here is the result:

*By 9.30 a.m. a baker seven miles away, who was unknown
to us, phoned, to say he had ninety-two large loaves made in
error—could we use them? The evening post brought in £8
(within 3d.), and the next morning the first cheque of £25
received for three months met the rates.*

Mr. Redwood also quotes from a letter written to him by Mr. Shearman, the evangelistic secretary of The Bible School and Missionary Association, Hampstead.

It is a rule of our work never to ask for money, but to leave our needs with God. Many times we have been in difficult places, but we have always been delivered.

One of the most notable instances occurred when, with only £200 in the bank, we had faith to purchase a church for £1,700. The amount in hand was paid as deposit, and the time came when it would be forfeited if the balance were not forthcoming on the morrow.

At bedtime no money had arrived, but the matter was completely committed to God, and Mr. Carter was about to retire for the night when he saw something lying on the front-door mat. As it seemed to be nothing but an advertisement in a cheap-looking envelope his impulse was to leave it there, but on second thoughts he picked it up.

It proved to contain £1,000 in notes, without a single word of explanation. The remaining £500 arrived the next morning, while the completion of the purchase was being held up at the solicitor's office for the want of it.

Could there, indeed, be more striking confirmation than this of the truth of the command to the Three Kings in the desert? That school which cancelled its standing orders and waited for God to act was obeying the command to act in confidence: *Thus saith the law, ye shall not see wind, neither shall ye see rain, yet make this valley full of ditches.*

Note carefully, however, that all these people were filled with a sense of purpose in life. They did not ask for Rolls Royces and a life of ease—imagine the folly of supposing that the Law has any concern with that sort of thing! No, the life that harnesses the power of the Law is the life that is dedicated to the mission of Truth in some degree, and which can rightly call upon the Fatherhood of God for support.

TELEPATHY
(The Master of Destiny)

(Based upon a lecture given at Brasenose College, University of Oxford, on the 14th February, 1934, also at The White Rock Pavilion, Hastings, April 9th, 1934, The Spa Theatre, Bridlington, January 26th, 1934.)

In the two previous chapters you have had revealed to you the startling fact that there is nothing impossible, as well as nothing new, under the sun; for, indeed, the powers of electricity and of machinery, of which the Western peoples are so proud, have been harnessed long ages ago by more subtle means than those now employed by us.

In the first lecture it was shown that all the powers of the anæsthetic, and of the electric crane* even, could be manifested by anyone who had developed their inner faculties—and all without the use of drugs or machinery.

In the second lecture it was shown that there is a law of spiritual cause and effect which puts to shame the childish manœuvrings of the average human mind. It was shown that all the "wire pulling" of the world to-day is childish as compared with the great Laws of the Universe by which all wrongs are righted and all accounts balanced and ruled off.

This lecture will show that there was telephony, telegraphy, broadcast and beam radio, radio-vision and picture-transmission long before the days of Hertz, Marconi and Baird.

In the depths of quiet, scented forests, where the peace and beauty of the world was an ever-present witness to the majesty of God (so different from the roar and tear of this so-called civilization), the Aryan Hindoos worked these

---

* *This is an allusion to levitation.*

things out long ago. They found that, as electricity is the most subtle interconnecting force known to Western science to-day, so the mysterious connection between mind and mind is the great primary force in all the manifestations of hypnotism and control of illusion.

CHAPTER THREE

IN the first lecture of this series I taught the meaning of the influence which one mind can exercise over another. In the second lecture I indicated how to get into touch with, and remain in contact with, the great Universal Mind in which we live and move and have our being.

In this lecture I am going to reveal to you the mysterious connection between all our minds and the Universal Mind.

Telepathy, according to the dictionaries, is derived from two Greek words meaning "thinking at a distance." But those who compiled the dictionaries did not know what telepathy really is, nor what it can do; and the Western dictionaries and reference books need complete revision on all these things relating to psychic science. There is more in telepathy than mere thinking-at-a-distance: for that would be no more powerful than a telephone message—apart from the power which every spoken word possesses. The power I am discussing is much more than this. It is the transmission of dynamic thought-power; the greatest power in the world; much greater than anything yet known to Western science. It is the Invisible Influence of which I have spoken in my previous lectures, and which forms the subject of one of my previous popular books* on these subjects.

It differs from all transmitted power, as understood by the Western scientists, for it is not a question of projecting a force over a certain distance, but of the total elimination of Space and Time. Space and Time do not exist except as the "ingredients of illusion"; they are the warp and the woof of the garment of *Mayâ* in which the Universal Mind is clothed for a while so that God may be manifest. Therefore, when we penetrate that illusion, we eliminate Time and Space, and find ourselves operating upon a plane where they have no meaning. Upon that plane there are no "miles per hour," for the unity of all things is realized.

Thus, by conquering Time and Space through the piercing of *Mayâ*, we achieve in quiet dignity all the things that the Western world achieves amid the stench of petrol fumes and burnt gases, and the crash of electric discharges.

The Aryan Hindoo Masters unravelled the secrets of this great power more than three thousand years ago. In the peace and quiet of

---

* *The Invisible Influence* (Rider & Co.), 5s. net.

their hills and forests they devoted centuries to the unravelling and the perfecting of their knowledge of the human mind and the methods for its control, whilst our forefathers were still barbarians in the forests, their woaded bodies tense with elemental fears. During the Indian Mutiny this force was used in its full power by these Adepts in the location of the English troops, and the British Government was baffled to know how the information could be known to the Aryan Hindoos long before the electric wire had transmitted it to themselves. They did not know that there are two worlds—one visible world which we *think* we know, and one invisible world which most of you take no heed of, though some of us know it even better than the world of the five senses.

But it is becoming easier to discuss these things with Westerners nowadays, and particularly since the advent of the wireless. People are quite prepared to admit that they never could have believed radio possible had they not heard it with their own ears. If wireless is possible, then it may be that even more wonderful things are also possible: in fact, wise men would now hesitate to draw a line between what is possible and what is impossible. All things are possible, and impossible is the adjective of fools.

Let us press to the full this analogy between radio and telepathy. In both cases there is a transmitter and a receiver, and the attainment of communication depends upon two instruments being completely in tune one with the other. How do we know that the human mind and body (the totality of the perceptible human organism) is not a sort of combined radio receiver and transmitter which is able to be tuned into the vibration of other instruments for the purposes of communication? It is an extraordinary thing, but the results shown by my instrument (the Cannon psychograph described in THE INVISIBLE INFLUENCE*) lend added weight to the above analogy, for they show that the mental reactions of two persons are identical whilst they are actually in telepathic communication: in other words, two people are in a state of mental harmony during the transference of thought between them. If two subjects are attached to my psychograph, independently and synchronously, it is possible, after one or two tests have been made, to test their mutual harmony and compare it with the degree of communication which can be achieved between them.

The psychograph records a separate chart of the actions and reactions of two persons connected to it, and it will be found that when two people succeed in demonstrating thought-transference they will, if attached to this instrument, cause it to record almost identical graphs. In the appendix to this chapter will be found two graphs given by Mr. A and Mr. T.

---

* *The Invisible Influence* (Rider & Co.), 5s. net.

These gentlemen were attached to the instrument independently and synchronously, and Mr. A was told to telepathize a thought to Mr. T. In the meantime the psychograph steadily recorded their reactions, rather as a tape machine records the movements of the Stock Market. In due course Mr. T told me what Mr. A had thought of, and the latter immediately confessed this to be correct. During actual thought transference their two charts were almost identical, as may be seen by the reader.

Now this demonstration proves that the minds of two people are in tune with each other during telepathic communication just as the aerial systems of the transmitter and receiver are in tune during wireless communication. It should be clearly understood, nevertheless, that a big difference exists between wireless communication and telepathy: for, whereas the wireless receiver must be tuned in to the transmitter before reception takes place, the brain of the telepathist can gain contact with the brain of the recipient by pure mental determining, or direction and concentration of thought-force. He tunes himself to the receiver instead of the reverse. Bear in mind this fact when we discuss Black Magic in a later lecture, for you will then realize that the way to escape from the toils of the Black Magician is to tune oneself so strongly to the vibration wavelength of Christ-power that the evil vibration (every wave is a vibration) cannot gain an echo in one's mind.

Another startling similarity between radio and telepathy lies in the fact that both can be transmitted more effectively after dark. It is said that the wireless waves, being vibrations of the same ether as that which carries the vibrations from the sun, are less interfered with when the solar vibrations cease to operate from sundown to sunrise: there is no undue interference during that period. Telepathy is transmitted by means of a still finer vibration of ether: and it is known that the sun sends out rays which change these etheric vibrations during the day, and so render telepathic communication more difficult. In the still of the night, telepathy can be practised even on those persons with whom the operator has no real conscious affinity. The potency of thought thus transferred is to some extent accounted for by the fact that the minds of most people are more passive during the dark hours of the night.

You will never understand all these things so long as you persist in looking at the universe as though it were a mass of inchoate forces. The universe is a unity: If that were not so it would not be a universe, for the very word "universe" means "centred around a single point." The universe we see is a series of reflections of the One Central Universal God, and all those reflections are, perforce, disposed around that which they reflect. Thus it is that the force manifested in the universe is the same force as that which wells up within us in the form of consciousness. There is complete identity between ourselves, our inner life, and the outer life of the universe. We are not separate from the universe; we are part of it, and because of that fact we are one with God Whose reflection it is, though we may allow our reflection to be dimmed by the shadow of evil—that illusion of illusions. This reflection is a reflection of thought, and it is by its invisible beams that we hold communion with the mind of God and, through Him, with all other creatures. Once we realize this fact we cannot have any doubt about the reality and the power of telepathy. We shall realize that telepathy not only exists, but *must* exist if the universe is to be a universe at all. In other words, telepathy is the invisible wire by which the Great God controls His living puppets on the stage of life.

The universe is filled with invisible thought-rays which are, as it were, magnetic currents connecting one person with another through the ether. Just as the intelligence which rules in the mind, can convey an idea to certain brain-centres and thence, through the agency of sensory nerves, can convey a command to the foot to raise itself, so, by exactly the same law, are the mind-currents or thought-waves sent out to others.

There is much evidence to suggest that the

human organism is indeed a very wonderful wireless set for picking up these invisible thought-waves. Few suppose, now, that thought is in the brain, or that memory is part of the brain. Surely the human brain, and especially the pineal gland contained therein, is like the structure of a wireless set? Is it not possible that the human brain is a receiving set for the waves sent out by that great broadcasting station, the Divine Mind? The brain of a man is an instrument for contacting with ideas and with the mental library of the past, the present and the future. To lose one's memory would mean to lose one's faculty for picking up the past, and a good memory would indicate a good faculty for picking up the vibration of the past. To be a clairvoyant means to be possessed of a similar faculty with respect to the future.

The clairvoyant can see a radiance surrounding the human head, not to mention that given off by the other mind-centres of the body referred to in the last chapter of this book. I can see halos, and the position and colour of these halos is intimately concerned with the mental nature and capacity of the person. Is it not possible that the halo is, humanly speaking, the normally invisible glow of that wonderful human wireless set—the brain? The reader must not take this illustration too literally; for no attempt has been made to give exact details of a human body as it appears to clairvoyant eyes. All that has been attempted here is to make the reader realize that there is a more wonderful truth in these powers than has ever been guessed by the purveyors of futuristic literature—whose covers are usually luridly filled with pictures of Martians with death-rays darting from their awful eyes.

The fact that the brain is less intimately associated with the mind than was at first thought, removes a whole mass of difficulties for the Western mind. During sleep, or under an anæsthetic, or even in hypnotic states, the mind and the brain are often not in association. This lends added weight to the suggestion that the brain is really a wonderful wireless set which is designed to pick up the transmissions of an unseen world. You will still think with your mind when your physical body and brain lie silent in the grave.

I sometimes speculate as to what sort of reality lies in the great etheric sea in which these vibrations are set up. I imagine what voices of life and death are "broadcasting" into this great sea. I wonder what awful responsibilities lie with man as he tunes in his own mind and the minds of others to pick up or reject these voices. I even query what madness really is. Is it but the mistuning-in of the human mind by a faulty brain receiving-set due to some accident of birth or misuse by the owner? My work and my experience with the insane, taken in conjunction with my experiments upon both the sane and insane, make me wonder whether the latter are not really, as they so persistently claim, picking up the voices of devils—Servants of the Underworld, who are broadcasting into the subtle ether of Mind. Who is in a position to judge? The superficial thinker may "pooh-pooh" this idea, and fly in the face of Christ's teaching as to the reality of the Demonistic nature of madness. I cannot help feeling that the insane man is really a kind of mistuned-in wireless set which is picking up these wrong, distorted vibrations of evil voices. I have often heard an insane man complain of these voices, and have heard him describe the visions he has seen of these servants of Darkness. In like manner, I have often put a perfectly sane man into a trance and have had him speak with these very same voices and describe the same visions of horror. Pause for a moment and think over these experimental facts! Are you going to learn by experience and try to understand that everything *means* something, and that *even a madman cannot be dismissed as just a madman*, but may hold, in that very perverted brain which you despise, a secret which can be turned to the good of the human race?

If good and evil, normality and abnormality, can so be proven to be the result of "bad tuning-in," then surely it is our duty to bend our efforts to the correct tuning of the human psyche! Did not Saint Paul say that *We wrestle not against flesh and blood, but against principalities*, *against powers, against the rulers of the darkness of this world. . . .* *

To fight against these evil forces, one must control the individual vibrations just as is done during hypnosis. If we can make a normal man see the same things, and hear the same things that an insane man hears and sees, then why cannot we persist in our endeavours to make the insane man become normal by a reversal of the process? To put it very simply, if we do not like the programme that is coming from Daventry, why do we not tune in to London or elsewhere? If devils can, as it were, get in by suggestion, surely they can be turned out of the innermost human consciousness also by suggestion; for what can be suggested into our consciousness may also be suggested out again.

It may be that the disharmony of life which we seem to pick up is really the interference caused by human "receiving sets" functioning out of harmony, just as the horrible distortion of a radio receiver may be due to an oscillating receiver somewhere near by; at the same time it must be borne in mind that the Powers of Darkness are a real force; of this there can be no doubt.

For this reason we should be careful of ourselves and guard our mental processes with great care. Perhaps it would be true to call the Holy Bible a great Text-Book of the human radio set, because it deals with the science of

* Ephesians, 6: 12.

tuning in to God's broadcasting station and of
tuning out all that is evil. The New Testament
particularly stresses the need for keeping our
minds and hearts clean, pure, and simple,
because like attracts like. It is a strange thing
that in this Western world of machinery we
have lost the art of looking after our mental
machinery which is the most delicate and
important of all. How many thousands of
young men are there in this country to-day
who nurse their sports cars and their wireless
sets like children, and yet who leave their
minds prey to any thought of pride, or passion
or selfishness that may come along in the maze
of telepathized vibrations in which we live?
They are not bad fellows!—excellent men, in
fact!—but just absolutely ignorant of the power
that is locked in their breasts; ignorant of their
power to resist or to entertain the thought-
forces which breed hatred, and disease, and
war—ignorant of the delicate machinery of
their own "inner radio."

But *you* are not so unwise. *You* will not be
swept off your feet by the mad telepathizing
of the world we live in—this distorted, mis-
leading, disappointing reflection of God's
beauty. You will try more and more every
day to guard your mind and heart from the
intrusion of these unwelcome "radio waves" of
thought. You will realize that the only safety
and the only strength is gained by tuning yourself to God's wavelength by holding in your

mind only good thoughts, kind thoughts, clean thoughts, and thoughts of love, meekness, and pity: never for one moment hating any man: never for one moment being unkind to anyone even in thought; never being deceitful, lustful, or malicious.

Once you have got on to God's wavelength you will gain a new strength and a new power for good over others. You will not be a mere cheap receiving set, open to all that may be floating around in the subtle ether of mind, but you will develop a power of selectivity beyond the wildest dreams of the radio-designer, for you will be able to distinguish between the most incredible shades of good and evil. Once in this state you will also be able to concentrate upon the real things of life—the things that matter. You will be a man set apart, and the power that you seek will be given to you, for you will begin to draw unto yourself the invisible power that is freely flowing from God. Jesus Christ demonstrated this in His life, for His greatest deeds were done after He had been alone upon the mountains or self-lost in the wilderness: (if you would be great you must think alone). There the virtue flowed into His pure consciousness like an unsullied stream, ready to be given out by Him to the sick and the sinful. Did He not say when the woman touched the hem of His garment: *Somebody hath touched me! for I perceive that virtue is gone out of me.* * Was not this virtue

* St. Luke, 9: 46.

of which Jesus spoke, the magnetic power (the divine Magnetism) with which He was filled by His true telepathic contact with His Father?

History records many persons who have possessed this power in a magnified degree, though, indeed, they have not always used it for the good of others. But these people have always been dominant characters: they have commanded men by the subtle emanation of their minds; by pure mental determining. They have been like human dynamos, simply surging with energy and power.

Take the case of Napoleon Bonaparte. He was cognizant of the magnetic power which he possessed, and was an excellent psychologist. It was he who used to describe the conscious, the subconscious, and the unconscious minds as "cupboards." "The first cupboard of the conscious mind," he used to say, "is open before my eyes. The second cupboard of the subconscious mind is closed, but I have the key. The third cupboard which represents my unconscious mind, is locked and I cannot see the contents thereof and I have no known key wherewith I can open it." Napoleon did not know that the telepathic power of the clairvoyant would have ransacked his unconscious mind and would probably have been able to reveal to the world what potent powers in the Kingdom of Darkness were using him telepathically to spread blood and fire over half the earth.

Mary Baker Eddy, the Founder of Christian Science, was just such another of these dominant personalities. She spent the greater part of her life in circumstances of poverty, ill-health and fear; but all the time, according to her biographers, she seems to have been wanting to know about occult matters. She seems to have knocked, and knocked, and knocked upon the door of knowledge often running away before the door was opened. This was the way in which she tuned-in her mind to do what it eventually did. For the greater part of her life she was blindly tuning-in her mind to any chance vibration which might come that way. Then, quite suddenly, she sprang into fame, and at an age when most women have settled down to become respectable grandmothers, she created an empire greater than that of Cæsar's. But she never quite controlled her own "radio receiving set" for she seems to have been haunted, even in her years of apparent triumph, by the ghastly fear that other people's minds were attacking her with the telepathic powers which she vaguely knew existed. She had three husbands, one of whom she divorced, and the last one died in circumstances which necessitated an autopsy. So powerful was the grip upon her mind of this ghastly power of misapplied telepathy (which she misnamed Malicious Animal Magnetism) that she refused to believe the verdict of the medical men, but maintained to the end her contention that her husband had died of arsenic administered mentally. Although I am a doctor of medicine, I cannot deny, in view of my knowledge of the greater power of the invisible influence, that Mrs. Eddy may have been right, and that the death of her husband may have been caused by the evil vibrations of thoughts which human minds spread about the world by distorting God's great broadcast of Life, Peace and Beauty. Most certainly the mind can destroy life by the projection of an idea of death. There is a cult in India which can wither trees at its command, and yea—life its very self— and I have related the intriguing story of the Black Magician of Surat* in THE INVISIBLE INFLUENCE, which proves the power of thought. You need not boggle at the strange idea of poison being administered mentally, as Mrs. Eddy suggested, for thought can easily influence the body so as to produce chemical and organic changes—whether telepathized or not. There is the case of a woman who saw a heavy weight fall upon her child's foot; she fainted, and, upon being restored to consciousness, was found to have a wound upon her own foot which was identical with that found upon that of her child. It was a real wound, too, for it went through the various stages of suppuration, and eventually healed by granulation of the tissue as in an ordinary wound.

Consider likewise the birth of a child. The

* An actual case recorded by a famous Judge in India.

processes of conception and gestation are quite unconsciously carried on. From where does the mother get the power to do this? Is it not that she is acting quite unconsciously as a sort of "picture receiver" and is building up the picture of her child in her body from the wave impulses telepathically received from a Central Broadcasting Station? God, the Creator, is transmitting the story of life, and the mother hears that story in her unconscious mind. So deep in the unconscious mind are these processes carried on, however, that the mother is quite unaware of what is happening; and has consciously no knowledge of the processes entertained by her unconscious mind.

It seems to be a *sine qua non* of all telepathic processes that the deeper they lie in the unconscious mind the greater is the elimination of all obstacles to their fulfilment, for the etheric vibrations of the Universal Mind have then undivided sway, with a potency so great as to be almost incredible of belief. One cannot imagine what would happen if the average expectant mother had a direct hand in the formation of her child. In fact, there are many examples of involuntary interference with the process through shock; mothers have received some rude mental impression before the birth of their child, and the intensity of the shock has gone below the surface of their minds and has interfered with the subtle workings there. The result has been some deformity of the child owing to the interruption of the incoming telepathic wave from the Universal Mind which is directing the growth of the child; just as a radio-picture might be spoiled by some local interference of even a temporary nature.

The fact that all these processes go on in the depths of the human unconscious mind is made clear by the fact that they can normally be "tapped," as it were, only by those people who are in hypnotic state, or trained and gifted "psychics," and also by the more astounding fact that the deeper the somnambulic state (that is to say, the deeper the trance state), the less important becomes the distance between the hypnotized subject and the person with whom he wishes to communicate. A subject in a light stage of hypnosis requires to be fairly close to the person whose thoughts he reads (yes, he can *read* the thoughts of others as easily as he can communicate his own), but as the trance becomes deeper and deeper, so the distance over which he operates can be lengthened without any difficulty whatsoever, until in the deep trance state the mind completely masters distance, and the factors of Time and Space do not exist. A person in a deep trance is in direct contact with the unseen world of thought and therein he will find every thought of earth's millions ready to be tapped by the master mind of man.

In The Invisible Influence, I recounted a story of how I lost a trunk during one of my journeys, and of the method whereby it was found for me by the assistance of a friend, who, passing into a deathlike trance, was able to locate the place where I had left it and then knock on the door of an official's house, hundreds of miles away and deliver a message asking for the trunk to be sent on: (the "Direct Voice" of Spiritualism). In the same book I related the placing of a certain British Colonel in a deep trance, and, whilst in that state, made him follow a certain eminent statesman for three whole hours, and at the same time also made him write down the movements, words and thoughts of that statesman in detail; to the amazement of the Colonel himself, and much to the horror of the statesman, when, at a later date, they were conscious of this experiment.

I know a man who is possessed of a peculiar ability in this direction, who awoke one night to see a friend of his standing at the foot of his bed. "What do you want?" he asked. "I can't sleep," complained the shadow at his feet. "Please send me to sleep!" Rising up in his bed and assuming a commanding air, my friend said in a loud voice: "Go to sleep, and do not awaken until nine o'clock!" The vision faded. When the two people met a few days later, they compared notes and found that all had happened exactly as they had experienced it. In this case, each knew of the other's powers, and the communication was quite deliberate and desired.

You can do this for yourself! Think of your friend, and picture his face in your mind's eye. If you find this difficult, then get a photograph and speak to it audibly. Concentrate your whole mind on your purpose and, just as you are falling asleep that night, keep your friend clearly in mind. If you carry out your end of the experiment with sufficient power you will find that you will succeed in conveying to your friend a sense of your nearness, and your desire, and if you want him to write a letter, you will find that a letter will arrive from him within a few days. I told you in an earlier chapter how to clothe your thoughts with matter! In a sense you are doing just that very thing by the potent use of telepathy.

Don't be deceived by the apparent realness, and the "everydayness" of the things which are real to your conscious mind. Remember that the conscious mind is but the outside wall of the Palace of the Unconscious, wherein are locked the treasures of Memory, Music, Language, Love and Life. You have the Golden Key to that palace in your own breast. It consists in the understanding of the telepathic nature of all knowledge and power. For, knowing this, you may re-shape your life, using your desires as the "tuning dials" by which to tune in the good waves of thought-power and cut out the evil ones.

Many of you, no doubt, tuned-in your wireless sets last Christmas to pick up the bells of Beth-

lehem, and heard their message of peace and
goodwill ringing out into the great sea of ether
in which the whole world swims. Similarly, no
doubt, you might have tuned in to some other
station and have heard a message of racial pride
and warlike sentiment being sown into that
same invisible field. Exactly thus it is with the
Universal Mind in which we live and move and
have our being; every thought we think and
every word we utter is sown into that world of
mind by telepathic communication, where it
echoes through the valley of time into eternity.
Others can tune into it, and hear it still echo,
and will be able to continue to do so, until the
the Great God of the Universe sends forth the
call that the ether shall be hushed. In that day
the great Karmic record will be liquidated,
and all that is fit to persist will remain, but all
that is evil, and vile, and contrary to the Law of
Love, will be silenced and hushed for ever.
This is what the Bible calls The End of the
World, and it is not far distant now (two or
three years); the Pyramids stop at 1936 and so
does all ancient Eastern prophecy. In that day a
man will be able to tune into this great
Universal Mind, and, no matter what wavelength his mind searches, will find only beauty
and joy and peace, for the evil things will
have been banished for ever from the ether of
the Universal Mind. Therefore, take great
heed of your thoughts that they be good
thoughts and not of evil. For it is certainly

true that those who cling to the evil thinking
of the world become at last a part of that evil
thought, and their unconscious mind becomes
linked permanently to that which must at last
be cast forth into Outer Darkness when the
Great God of the Universe purges the Universal
Mind of all evil.

Let us, then, no longer be fools, but let us
learn to understand the art of Living. Let us
understand that the whole duty of man is to
gain control of his own "tuning-in" and to
harness the Good and reject the Evil.

One thing we see clearly as we go on in our
study of the mind in the light of this great power
of telepathy, and that is the reality of the
invisible influence which pervades our whole
life; we can see that there is a real God and a
real Devil, each ceaselessly fighting for the possession of our unconscious mind, our SOUL,
which will survive our body after death. Therefore, whilst you have the power to tune-in your
own mind, select the wavelength of God with
all your heart. The Science of telepathy is the
philosophy of how mind can influence mind;
and mind is the greatest force we know of in
this world in which we live. You are anxious
to know more of this greater and, to many of
you, still unseen world. Remember that the
law of attraction and repulsion is operative in
all worlds.

As regards knowledge: Ask *and ye* SHALL
receive; Seek *and ye* SHALL *find;* Knock *and the*

door SHALL *be opened.* * May I, in closing, emphasize that you must knock on the RIGHT door, opened in response to the vibrations of your own Soul, in accordance with your own desires.

Good music vibrates with your very soul-vibration and releases it from imprisonment, making wonderful things seem possible and easy of accomplishment, for its telepathic power is beyond our ken.

Telepathy is the forerunner of things made real. A thought sooner or later becomes a thing: do not the scriptures speak of *the word made flesh.*†

A thought in your mind is so powerful that it will telepathize itself again and again to your unconscious mind until it becomes YOU! Heed this great truth! How great is the power of a single thought! Therefore man should make an art of thinking. Man's thoughts depend largely upon the books he reads, the things he sees, and the friends with whom he associates, and his visible and invisible environment. We grow like those with whom we live!

The master thinker is an artist and is careful to paint only the Divine designs upon the canvas of his mind. He paints these pictures with masterly strokes of power and decision, having perfect faith that there is no power to mar their perfection and that they shall manifest in his life, the ideal made real.

---

* Matthew 7 : 7 (paraphrase).
† John 1 : 14.

THE CANNON PSYCHOGRAPH

The Cannon Psychostethokyrtographmanometer, or Psychograph, or Thought Recording machine, is an instrument for recording the minute breathing movements of a subject and for making a graph of the nature of the thoughts passing through the patient's mind.

As has been explained in the foregoing article, the relation between breathing and thought is a most intimate one, and it is upon this relationship that the value of the Cannon Psychograph depends.

The instrument consists of a delicate and complex rubber fitment which is placed round the subject's chest and abdomen and secured there by light bronze chains. The breathing movement of the subject's chest and abdomen causes the delicate rubber fitment to be compressed and released, whereupon the air contained in it is equally compressed and released. The varying air pressures are conveyed through suitable rubber and glass tubing to an air chamber and there are made to cause a rise or fall in a water-level which, in its turn, moves a light float up and down in tune with the subject's breathing. The float is fixed to one end of a light rod upon the other end of which a suitable recording pen is fitted. The pen thus moves up and down on the paper in phase with the subject's breathing and, owing to the rotary movement of the paper cylinder, the result is a perfect graph of the subject's respiratory movements.

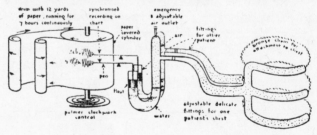

The above diagram sets out the main parts and operations of the Psychograph. The production of the two graphs (two subjects being attached to the machine at one time) is shown in progress on this purely diagramatic sketch. The graphs of Mr. A. and Mr. T. referred to in the foregoing article are reproduced here, and the remarkable coincidence of the two independent graphs whilst actual thought-transference is in progress may be seen. The periods during which telepathy was in progress are clearly marked on the graphs which are produced side by side simultaneously on the one machine.

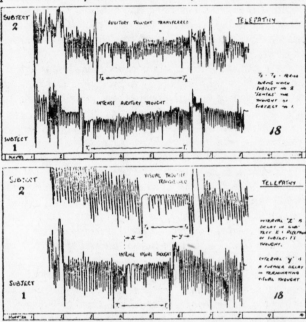

These graphs show quite clearly when the achievement of telepathic thought-transference took place, as witness the similarity of the two graphs in the portions T1 and T2

FAITH HEALING
(The Power of the Imagination)

(Based upon a talk given by the author as Guest of Honour at the Mayfair Hotel on Sunday, March 4th, 1934, upon the occasion of a lecture by Mr. J. D. Beresford the novelist, and author of CAMBERWELL MIRACLE, a novel concerning faith-healing.)

A steam-engine cannot mend its own broken mechanism because it is a creation of the human mind—a procreation in which the mind of its creator does not live. It has no self-consciousness, but depends upon its creator's direct action for its healing.

But a man is not like a steam-engine, and those who have tried to disprove faith-healing by likening man to a machine are utterly wrong in their premises and must be wrong in their conclusions.

In man the spirit of the Creator of all Life is manifested by reflection. In man the divine Flame glows and warms all the parts of the outward man whom we erroneously call physical.

This Flame is all potent to give life and to preserve it and to restore it, but so long as man insists upon treating his body as though it were a lump of mechanism, so long will his body answer to that picture, for thought is more than a mere commentary—it is dynamic. It does not merely observe facts, but creates them. It does not trail at the heel of the body but leads it.

This fact explains the reality of faith-healing, which in a sense is wrongly named, for it is not faith that does the healing but the power of God which flows into us through the channels which faith has opened. We have to live and to think and to act in conscious understanding that we are channels of God's universal Life, and once we let this fact take possession of us we become filled with the divine Fire.

Faith-healing puts the horse in front of the cart of life once more. It is a part of that resurgence of spiritual power which is making itself felt in the world. It is the expression in the world of medicine of the belief that the body is more than meat and raiment, and that it is in fact the Temple of the Holy Spirit and the Living Garment of God in the shape of man.

CHAPTER FOUR

I HAVE listened with great interest to Mr. Beresford's excellent analysis of "What is Faith-Healing?" and my interest has been strengthened by my great sympathy for him in his struggle against his own infirmity, and moreover I have been warmed greatly by the unselfishness of his attitude towards the whole question. He is not a bigot who, having stumbled across some measure of relief for himself, wishes to publicize his own good fortune: on the contrary, he only thought of trying to cure himself because it dawned upon him that he could not preach a gospel of hope to others unless he himself were a living example of the power of that gospel. Greater love has no man than this, that he forget his own welfare in the welfare of others.* Surely that is a permissible paraphrase of a well-known biblical saying. Love is certainly the essential ingredient in all

---

* John, 15:13. *Greater love hath no man than this, that a man lay down his life for his friends.*

true living, for without it even faith is void, and knowledge is of less than no account. Did not Paul truly say: . . . *though I have the gift of prophecy, and understand all mysteries, and all knowledge : and though I have all faith, so that I could remove mountains and have not charity, I am nothing.* *

One thing Mr. Beresford said during his talk which gives me an opportunity of making these words of mine something more than a mere formal occasion, and that was his avowal of a life-long interest in "the way things work." He is not content with believing that a thing happens and can happen. He wants to know why it happens so that he may be sure that it will happen again.

This is a very right and a very worthy motive on his part. For it was just this lack of knowing "why things happen" that has lost so much vital knowledge to the world over countless centuries. Why, here in England, just a few centuries gone, faith-healing was an accepted fact. Even to-day, you will find people in the country districts who will cure warts by faith-healing—yes, it is faith-healing even though it does pin its faith to the knocking of a stone off a gate. But no one ever explained the action of the mind upon the body, nor gave an adequate explanation of the power of thought. Instead of having knowledge, the people pinned their faith in blind fashion upon

---

* 1 Corinthians 13 : 2.

the mere whim, as it were, of God, or of Jesus Christ, or of the Virgin Mary, to whom medieval England uttered up its prayers. They gave themselves up to a belief in a lawless universe, where things sometimes happened and sometimes did not. They did not know of a law of Karma, or of the power of thought. They did not know "how things happen" in the unseen universe of God, and so they lost the power to heal and gave themselves up to a blind belief in a mechanical universe wherein man's body was like a cog in an engine.

Mr. Beresford may be grateful for having this desire to know how things work allied to a love for his fellow-men, for together these emotions indeed work miracles. They help a man to find knowledge, and, what is even more important, they teach him how to use his knowledge when he has got it.

It is my duty and my privilege to be able to tell you that this emotion of love expressed in a desire to heal by faith is not a mere sentimentality which finds no place in a universe of law. For, indeed, health is a primary law of the universe, and it means WHOLENESS—which is the first thing necessary to the existence of a universe. The very word "Universe" means "situated around a common centre," and it is not difficult to see that you cannot have a common centre without having wholeness, or health.

Once you see this fact and see it clearly, you are on your way to complete health. You will immediately begin to perceive that you are part of a whole, and that your own body is a little "whole" to which many parts belong. Now, if you are in harmony with God's unseen and larger "Wholeness," then you begin to pattern in your own body the results of that harmony. Just as the painter reproduces upon his canvas a little miniature of the mighty mountain. If the painter saw the mountain as a frowning crag then his picture would be harsh and foreboding. But if he saw it as a sunlit spire, then his picture would be inspiring and radiant of hope. So with your life. If you look upon the universe as a wilderness of hurtling planets, violent eruptions, and material inexorability, then you will hold thoughts of harshness and your life will be set about by the demons of fear, distrust, and doubt. You will begin to need to protect yourself from other men, and from that philosophy breed all the war and the ill of the world. Yes, the ills of the world all spring from the paralysing effect of fear. Not only ill-health, but financial failings, moral failings and spiritual failings, all spring from the ignorance of the true nature of Life and its Law. These things begin with imagination. It is the imagination that must be controlled. So many people look upon the imagination as a sort of brain lobe, but really it is a process—the process of forming an image in the mind.

It is this image that forms our character and

our life. If we imagine a universe of light and power then our lives will become moulded in such a way to make us fit inhabitants of that universe. If we, on the contrary, imagine a universe wherein Good and Evil are *equal*, we shall manifest fear, and doubt and all the characteristics which an inhabitant of such a universe would find natural.

Let us, then, deal with this process of imagination. Let us take a grip upon it and make it work for us, and for our health and our good. Let us see the law operating behind this faith-healing force of which we hear so much. Let us no longer look upon it as odd, or weird, or peculiar. It is nothing of these. It is a real law, and a real force. There is only one way of dealing with the imagination, and that is to "make-believe," as it were. We have to "pretend" that what seems to us unreal is actually very real. If we are ill we have to make health a reality to us. Only in this way will the forces of Life leap up in us and repair the damage to our body. As Mr. Beresford told you, a crab can grow a new claw if one is severed. A man cannot grow a new leg. Why not? Simply because the crabby mind works in such a way that the growth of a new claw is natural to it, but the mind of man has rejected the possibility. Change the thought—really and truly change it to the deeps of the unconscious mind—and the man will grow a new leg as easily as the crab grew a new claw.

How few people have realized the hidden meaning of Christ's great saying: *Except ye become as little children, ye shall not enter into the kingdom of heaven.** In other words, except you have enough faith to be able to see the good things about you and to believe them real, ye shall not attain to those good things. Did I not say in a previous lecture that this world is an illusion—a vision in a looking-glass, as it were? Did I not tell you how a man may attain to the control of illusion? Is not this faith-healing just that process? Do we not control illusion and make our bodies conform to the perfect picture we hold in our mind?

The little child is perfect at making these illusions. It is an adept at "let's pretend." It unconsciously takes the first step in all creation —the control of the imagination.

All the bad conditions prevalent in the world to-day are due to what may be called a disease of the imagination. We have allowed our imaginations to get out of our control, because nobody has believed the power that lies in them. Men have gone on believing that they may think anything they like in private, and that, so long as their thoughts are not known, they will be safe. Fools! They have not realized that the unconscious mind holds a perfect record of every hidden thought and of every hidden desire. They have not understood that their materialistic thoughts will ravage

* Matthew, 18: 3.

their bodies with disease, their nations with war, their businesses with depression, and their morals with corruption. They have not realized that in the unseen world they are heaping up for themselves a load of debt that cannot be paid except by suffering, or by repentance and reformation. Their imaginations have got out of their control, because they have not realized the need for guarding their action.

Do not suppose that a man need hold definite thoughts of sickness in his mind to enable him to become sick. Not at all. It is enough for him to think of his body as a machine that is in danger of disease. The thoughts of sickness are implicit in the first thought and they will manifest. Therefore, it is not enough for a man to go through life with no control of his imagination. He must take himself in hand, otherwise, if he does not control himself, evil forces will do so. Your thoughts will become things, and a disordered mind will make a disordered life and a disordered body. Illness is not a positive thing but a negation of wholeness. It is the result of bad thinking or of no thinking.

Have you grasped this simple law? It is the "why and the wherefore" of Mr. Beresford's faith-healing. What others make such a mystery of, I reveal to you as the result of a clear law. Therefore, tell yourself this fact over and over again. Do not get slack about it. As you concentrate upon it you will find your mind will more readily hold the right thought. Just as it becomes easier to swim or to ride a bicycle after much practice, so does it become easier to be a good liver by practice. School yourself to hold great thoughts. Make your imagination fasten upon good things, great things, noble things. Make a perfect picture of health in your imagination, and it will cause you to tune closer into the harmonious wavelength of God. Health will come to you! The simple act of make-believe will work the miracle—in Camberwell or anywhere else, Mr. Beresford.

Do you know that it is possible to develop the muscles of your body by practising imaginary exercises? Try it, and see for yourself. Lie in bed at night and give your mind up for ten minutes to the conjuring up of a picture of some simple exercise, such as the exercising of the arm muscles or the calf muscles. Go through the exercises in your mind: picture yourself doing them. Concentrate upon them with all your might, at the same time taking in deep breaths. Do this for a fortnight and see if the muscles have not been improved by the imaginary exercises. This is quite obvious when you come to think about it. Why do you suppose that the muscles improve by ordinary physical jerks? Because of the action of the body? Nonsense! The muscles of a corpse would not improve, no matter how much they were forcibly exercised. No, the physical jerks constitute a little mental ritual which impresses the imagination with the importance of the muscles, and with the general health of the body, and this causes the muscles to rise in response to the need of the body. It does not matter whether that need is expressed by physical action or not: so long as you get the impression on the mind with sufficient intensity, you will get the effect you desire.

The same thing applies if you are feeling "down in the mouth," as the saying goes, and need fresh air and sunshine. Perhaps time and pressure of work will not enable you to get them. Very well then. Lie down, or sit fully relaxed in an easy chair, and imagine you are lying naked on the seashore, with the fresh ozone acting upon every pore of your skin, your lungs full of the fresh sea breezes, and the sun pouring out upon you its life and power. Keep this picture steadfastly in mind for fifteen minutes, and keep the body relaxed and the lungs quietly and powerfully functioning. At the end of that time you will feel as fit as if you had been lying on a beach for hours in the manner in which you imagined it.

You will be astounded at the result you will obtain from this most simple of imaginations. Try it for yourself! It will do you good. But do not half believe in what you are doing: play the game according to the rules, and enter into the exercise with all your heart and soul.

These simple exercises of the imagination

are the basis of the secret of life. Control your imagination: hold in it only those things that are good and desirable, then throw all your mental power behind these desires, and your life will shape itself accordingly. How could it be otherwise? The product must always take on the shape of the mould. Your life is the product of the mould of your imagination: therefore guard it!

People do not stop to realize that even the most materialistic among us really admit the truth of living on faith. The very man who proudly claims that he is "a man of common sense, who has no time for faith," will quite naturally pay his money into the bank and draw a cheque upon it because he has faith that the money will be credited to his account. "Credited to his account—" why the very word CREDIT means faith, and it is quite the thing nowadays to hear people say that the world lives on credit. If only the world would be logical about it we should quickly arrive at the millenium. If people would only carry their faith to the Nth degree and believe in themselves, their God, and their fellow-men, we should leave the economic system to clear itself up; for the political system, as the human system of man's body, lives by faith.

You didn't create your own body, your parents did not create it either: they were merely agents for Life. Life created your body, and Life will heal it when it goes wrong if only

you will open the way for Life by keeping your
mind in the path of faith. You do not cause the
wheat to grow, nor do you control the rains
and the harvests, yet many of us believe that
we can control our supply of God's good things.
The truth is that if we only had faith in God,
we should not "lay up for ourselves treasure
on earth where moth and rust doth corrupt,"
but we should "lay up for ourselves treasure
in heaven" by having faith that next year will
bring new harvests for distribution among all
men. But men have no faith. They keep
thinking fearful thoughts—what will happen
to me to-morrow? What will happen if another
nation does this or that? How shall I live if I
lose my job? This is entirely the wrong direction of your imagination. You should not concentrate upon morbid thoughts of that nature.
You do not need to worry about to-morrow,
or the minute after next, or the hour after next.
All you need to do is to concentrate on YOUR-
SELF at the present moment: watching carefully
that your own thoughts are right—NOW: being
meticulous in the observance of the right
attitude towards the problem of the moment:
THINKING THE RIGHT THING NOW: SAYING THE
RIGHT THING NOW: and DOING THE RIGHT
THING NOW, to the utmost of your ability.

Work well and rest well—these are the secrets
of success: and you cannot do either unless you
have attained to that inner peace which faith
in God alone can induce. When you work you

should do what you have to do with all your heart and with all your soul. Do not slacken because you do not like your job. Visualize the sort of job you want to satisfy your ideal, but at the same time work all the harder at your present one. This will set the laws of life in motion and you will assuredly get the job you desire. If, on the contrary, you have got the job you like, then buckle into your job in such a way that those who are above you will be bound to notice you. Do not be sly about it. Do not do your work well just for effect, or to be noticed of others. No, obey the commands of Jesus and pray in secret so that God who sees all things in secret shall reward you openly. In this way you will render to Cæsar (your present status) the things that it demands, and to God you will render faith and the praise of your heart which will reward you after a greater or a shorter while. You do not need to render homage to any man. Do your duty to all men because they also (whether rich or poor, good or bad) are sons of God, but render homage to God and reverence Him. If you preserve this true balance you will COMPEL YOUR SUPERIORS TO NOTICE YOU, because you will not offend them by affecting to despise them, nor will you revolt them by your obsequious manner. You will appeal to them as a MAN, and you will get your reward.

I cannot impress upon you too forcibly the fact that all this depends entirely upon yourself.

You want to be of some account in the world: in your profession; in your trade! Begin to play-act the part. Live it! Make it a part of yourself. It is up to you to begin to move the life-forces in your favour, for nobody else will do it for you. Imagine yourself as being what you want to be, and the faith behind this imaginative effort (for it is a supreme act of faith—creating in yourself the substance of things hoped for, as Paul says) will bring them to pass. The job you desired: the rank you wished to attain: the post you wanted to fill: the rôle you longed to act—all these will be yours if you act them in faith and in complete earnestness of purpose and with no levity in your mind.

A word of warning to you in this respect, however. In gauging your own importance do not allow yourself to float along in a sea of superlative egotism. More commonly speaking, do not let your head swell. A proper estimate of oneself must include a survey of one's short-comings: a realization of one's infinite task of self-development, and a clear understanding that the enormity of the task is no cause for regret or despair, but rather is a cause of great joy to think that one has such a clear road ahead of one, and such a clear law of progress along it. You must also realize the relative nature of your position, and thereby retain a proper balance and a proper self-control. The more you realize your own importance, the more you will need to realize how frail you

are except for the Life which is supporting
you—the Life which is God. This realization
will cool your self-esteem and put it into its
proper place. It will show you that, as a Son
of God, you are bigger than you ever dreamed
you could be, and you will find undreamed-of
greatness and depths of power in yourself: but
it will also show you that, as a "lone hand"
fighting a supposedly lone fight against the
universe, and puffed up with your own little
conceits, you are smaller than the poorest
and meanest of God's creatures. Another
thing you must consider, and that is the
question of proper rest for mind and body.
If you do not rest you cannot work properly,
and if you cannot work properly you will
never win success. Before you fall asleep at
night (begin this very night to control your
sleeping state), let every muscle of your body
go flabby. Think of all these muscles as huge
factories, employing millions of cell-men, and
actually tell them to knock off their labours and
take a rest. Most people go to sleep with their
muscles taut—all the cells keyed up and
waiting for the body to resume its work, just as
though they were workers in a factory who
never were allowed to go home and enjoy
relaxation but were always kept in the factory
by night and by day, ready to go on duty
again. Think what a terrible strain such
conditions would impose upon the workers!
They would soon break down in mind and

body under the strain. In the same way do
the little microscopic workers of the body need
rest and peace if they are not to break down
under the strain of life. When you have
learned to "send all your workers home" you
will be in a perfect state of relaxation. Your
legs will lie in effortless ease upon the bed;
your body will be in perfect peace, and your
head will be loosely connected to it—for your
neck muscles will all be "off duty." Now
breathe deeply and evenly, remembering what
I related in a previous lecture about breath-
control, and keep vividly in your mind the
picture you desire to materialize in your life-
experience. Think of the job you desire to
attain to: the love you wish to gain: the rank
you wish to hold: the duty you wish to under-
take. Then, still fully relaxed and breathing
deeply, you will fall asleep with this picture
held firmly in your mind. In the morning you
will awaken in a happy frame of mind: ready
to work well, and in absolute certainty that the
day will arrive when your dreams will come
true. Your certainty will be based upon truth—
for, indeed, your dreams must come true.

I have just been extremely thrilled and
interested by seeing the Italian proofs of my
book, THE INVISIBLE INFLUENCE, and to notice
that the Italian word for INFLUENCE is IN-
FLUENZA. Does that not make a powerful
appeal to you? Can you not see that the name
of that dreaded scourge which carried off

millions of people towards the end of the Great War is really indicative of its nature, and of the nature of all disease.* Does it not emphasize what I have been declaring in all these lectures? That disease is due to the action of an invisible influence (influenza) which telepathically affects the body through the mind.

We are surrounded by an etheric ocean in which the powers of thought move like lightning flashes from one mind to another. We are like complex instruments moving through a sea of power: our instruments flashing power one to another; being controlled by past influences from the power-house of memory to which all our instruments are tuned; and to the power-house of custom (the collective mind) to which we are likewise attuned. Sometimes waves of adverse power come to us and cause our instruments to jar and to disintegrate. Some-

---

* It should be borne in mind that the high *vibrations* of red transmitted-light will, if played upon the eyes for a period of half an hour, remove the symptoms of influenza. This shows very clearly the vibratory nature of disease. The East has taught for years that many "diseases," and especially INFLUENZA, enter the body through the eyes and not through the nose and throat. Influenza infection is not achieved, as so many people suppose, through the mouth or the nose, but actually takes place through the eyes. From the eyes the infection passes down the lachrymal duct into the nose and thence to the throat. In this connection it is interesting to remember that the eyes are especially troubled by this virulent dis-ease. Further corroborative evidence of the truth of these statements may be gathered from the fact that even bacteriologists now no longer believe Influenza to be caused by the *Bacillus Pfeiffer* (1892), or *Bacillus Influenza*. The reader must take these truths to heart so that he may the more appreciate the force of my statements concerning the relation of bacteria to disease, which he will find in the last chapter of this book.

times this jarring effect spreads to others and causes an epidemic of jarring and of disintegration. Then we say there is a plague, or an epidemic. Whether we call it INFLUENZA or not it is still INFLUENCE by mental unseen waves of thought.

But in the midst of all this chaotic action and reaction we have one haven of peace and strength that never changes. This is the great power-house of the universe: the great Universal Mind, God, the Creator of all things Who rules His universe by telepathic control. We need only to tune our instruments to His wavelength, and then all the other jarring waves are blotted out and effaced by His peace which truly passeth all understanding.

How do you tune into His wavelength? Why, I have been telling you all along! FAITH! and again, FAITH . . . faith that God is Good and that all the host of heaven and of earth must move to an increasing purpose when it is consciously attuned to His power. Try it and see the results. They are unfailing, for God never fails us!

BLACK MAGIC
(The Power of an Evil Thought)

(Based upon a lecture given in the Ballroom of The Mayfair Hotel, London, on the 13th May, 1934.)

Every single thing in the world has an opposite. Every Good has its possible Evil: every Positive has an opposite Negative: every good power may be turned to evil ends.

So it is with the powers of the mind. The great power of good which the thoughts of men can influence, have a sinister and opposite power of evil, and it is this evil power which we know in the East as Black Magic.

Black Magic signifies the destructive use of mental power. It is the misuse of spiritual development—for, contrary to popular ideas, spiritual things are by no means always good things.

This article states what Black Magic can do, and reveals the unseen powers that are spurring the world on to madness and evil—not only causing individuals to be evil, but also brewing collective evil out of the uncontrolled telepathic forces which individual evil releases.

Black Magic is a terrible blight, a ghastly curse, and the power of that curse is everywhere. Men sicken and die under the curse laid upon them: nations bleed and suffer beneath its spell.

Wake up! Peoples of the earth. Do not blame others for the sins that beset you! Look at your own hearts and minds! Therein lie the secret springs of all your troubles, and of the woes of this suffering world.

There are Black Magicians in the world who are deliberately carrying on their terrible work. But there are also millions and millions of ordinary people who are busy laying grievous burdens upon the world and upon their fellow-men, by constantly holding thoughts of anger, hatred, lust and envy. These people need to know the devastating work they are so effectively doing.

He that hath ears to hear, let him hear!

CHAPTER FIVE

THOSE who believe that we live in a universe of "solid matter" will find Black Magic difficult to believe. One sympathizes with them when one remembers that so great a man as the late Lord Kelvin once said that, "One half of hypnotism is fraud and the rest is bad observation." If great minds may be thus deluded, then we must not be too harsh in our condemnation of the populus who have no time to go deeply into such matters. But although one may sympathize with these unbelievers, one cannot, must not, dare not, desist from calling to them with all one's might and main to awaken and realize the evil that is in their midst; an evil that is creating sin, disease, war, and a host of evils whose source is little understood.

You men and women of common sense! You who think that the world is a good solid place where only comfortable things like money, pleasure, and personal safety are of any account: you must begin to open your eyes and understand that you live in a world of spiritual forces; you must begin to be aware of the forces that are operating all around you, for you are (like one of those wireless-controlled battleships), guided by unseen forces. You must begin to see that your comfortable, solid world is not so solid as you thought. It is a reflection of God in the screen of *Mayâ*. It is a living vortex of telepathic forces which are aiding you or harming you according to your own reception or rejection of the powers of Good and Evil.

Don't shut your mind to the mental nature of the universe as the late Lord Kelvin shut his mind to the facts of hypnotism. What Lord Kelvin denied so strongly a generation ago, is now a fact of Western medical science, and what I am broadcasting to-day will likewise be known to EVERYONE in a few years' time—unless the evil thinking of men and women has destroyed civilization in the meantime.

Be open-minded! Jesus, the great Nazarene *Yogi*, said, *Except ye be converted, and become as little children, ye shall not enter into the kingdom of heaven.** Meaning that your mind must be as open as the mind of a child. Unless your minds are open to facts you will see what you want to see and no more; you will be biased and deceived. You will make yourself believe what it suits you to believe. You will miss the point of life, and stagger amid the contending forces of the invisible world, and so bring ruin

* Matthew, 18 : 3.

and pain upon yourself and upon others. Remember that a man who believes in a material world shuts his mind to anything contrary to that conception so that, in the end, he is not able to believe even the evidence of his own eyes.

I do not want to make you afraid of the powers of evil, because fear opens the mind to the thoughts of the evil worker as surely as faith closes up the mind against him: but I desire to prevent you from being blind to the reality of this power.

I do not wish you to pooh-pooh it and so remain all the time a prey to it: I want to show you that there is a real reason why you should keep your mind tuned-in to Good, and why you should not think evil. A thought in your mind is so powerful that it will telepathize itself again and again to your unconscious mind until it finds a permanent echo there and so begins to shape your life. Imagine, then, what terrific power is generated if your evil thinking, or slack thinking (the idle thought), is also being supplemented by the similar thoughts of others!—remember that like attracts like. Imagine the hatred piling up in the invisible world between the nations—hatred which unless it is dispersed must sooner or later burst into a ghastly mess of bloodshed and horror. It is just like watching a great thunderstorm being brewed in the upper atmosphere, unseen to human eyes, where the forces are slowly piling up until they reach bursting-point.

In the visible world we see only how a man is *acting*, but in the invisible world there is growing up a thought-form associated with him, and it is this thought-form—this pattern in his unconscious mind—that will prove master in the end, and his real thoughts will be shown up, no matter how contrary to them his actions may be at present.

Ever since the publication of my book, THE INVISIBLE INFLUENCE,* I have had shoals of letters on the subject of Black Magic. Here is an extract from a letter received from the wife of an ex-Consul General of Italy. She writes: "In the East, my husband, the late Commander X, knew of facts regarding this evil: facts which he related to me, viz.—That if an envious person admired a child and caressed it, that child would either die or some evil would overtake it. So much were its parents or guardians persuaded of this fact that the child in question was immediately exorcized according to their rites and ceremonies. . . . Before concluding my letter I will just mention a fact that occurred to myself many years ago, when I was too young to have had either time or inclination to tackle deep subjects. I was in the Italian Maremma—between Tuscany and the Roman States, and this happened during the period of my first marriage with a then

* Rider & Co., London. 5s. net.

conspicuous and powerful magnate in the Province. Without any apparent reason I gradually became weak and nervous. My colour, which was normally of a healthy pink hue, entirely disappeared. I became so thin that the fact was remarked upon by all. I had no illness whatsoever, and was not lacking in any luxury or comfort. One day a lady called upon me: I knew her only slightly but she asked me to listen to her and to take her advice. *You are gradually dying without any apparent reason*, she said: *You are the victim of envy. The women of this citadel and of the Province envy you and your position, your beauty and your accomplishments, and also the fact that you are English, whereas an Italian lady has more right to be in your place.* Then she proposed my going to my dressing-room where she shut the door and prepared a basin of water. She poured some oil on the water, saying prayers and gesticulating with signs. At last she said, *Now you are free from the effects of the evil eye—evil wishing and influence. You will see that you will soon be better and become yourself again.* I just tolerated the performance—in reality not taking part in it, but it so happened that my health and general state of being rapidly improved; also events happened favourably for me and I lived to enjoy peace and happiness. This lady's prayers, faith, and goodwill seemingly prevailed."

Now I am quite aware that there are several

possible reactions to such a letter. The most popular one in the West just now would be to dismiss it as what is conveniently called "primitive superstition." (Just how much that sort of attitude is worth is shown by my story of Lord Kelvin's dismissal of hypnotism.) Another possible reaction to this lady's letter would be to get into a state of fear. This would be dangerous as it would open the mind to the power of evil. The only balanced reaction, because it is the only one that recognizes all the facts, is to admit that Black Magic does exist, but to be unafraid of it. We should recognize the truth about this unseen evil influence which is the cause of ruined lives, collapsing civilizations, and bad trade. For sin, sickness, and suffering are the result of careless, idle or bad thinking. As stated in a previous lecture, you must either run your own unconscious mind, or someone else will manage it for you: you must keep your "wireless set" tuned-in to the vibrations of Life, otherwise evil will get in.

Apropos of the danger of fear, THE YORKSHIRE EVENING PRESS of October 3rd, 1933, contains an article which is less interesting for what it says than for what it omits to say. After reporting the secretary of the Egypt Exploration Society as saying that . . . *there is no fear among the Egyptologists* (of the 'Evil Eye' of old Egypt) *and no difficulty in finding men, and women, for the expeditions to the land of the tombs*, the article goes on to point out that the Hon.

Richard Bethell, Lord Carnarvon, Sir Archibald Douglas Reid, Mr. H. G. Evelyn White, and an American society woman, have *all died* after having been connected either directly or indirectly with the excavations among the tombs of Ancient Egypt. *Mr. Evelyn White, indeed, committed suicide, actually saying that the curse was on him.* What is so interesting about the article is the way in which it tacitly confirms the contentions I am making: to wit, that those who do not fear the curse, because their disbelief is so positive and downright, are those who escape it; whereas those who have in their minds the slightest seed of doubt (as Mr. White obviously had) are those who tune-in to the curse; and upon these unfortunate people it will work its ghastly power. It just needs a little chink in your armour. It will do the rest. Once again, I say unto you—I am not an alarmist because the evil is here in our midst. We must awaken to the fact.

In the last lecture I spoke of Mrs. Eddy the Christian Scientist and told you how terribly afraid she was of this "Malicious Animal Magnetism" as she incorrectly named it. Now let me tell you the story of one of her followers who was accused of using that same power for her own ends. This woman was Mrs. Augusta Stetson, and the story concerning her reads as follows:

"When a prominent member resigned from the church after openly expressing his own hostility, his wife soon died. It was then whispered that Mrs. Stetson and her students had united to direct malicious animal magnetism against the unfortunate woman. Another woman in the church was firmly convinced, according to lurid accounts published in the New York Press, that Mrs. Stetson had filled her husband with malicious mental currents, but she went on attending the church regularly because she felt in fear for her own life. One member whose misfortune it was to enter into a dispute with Mrs. Stetson left the church, opened up an independent practitioner's office, and immediately went insane. He was carried to the asylum loudly declaring that Mrs. Stetson's malicious animal magnetism had broken him in mind and body. And eventually there were several suicides which some critics attributed to a fear of Mrs. Stetson's mental wrath.

"According to newspaper reports, these malicious mental treatments were carried on in much the same way that Mrs. Eddy had taught her students in the old College days. Mrs. Stetson would assemble her practitioners at noon of each day except Sunday. The lesson would be read aloud, and then the leader would announce the name of the person who was believed to be attempting to harm Mrs. Stetson and her work.

"'He does not want to harm the church,' the leader would announce aloud.

"Immediately all practitioners present would take up his thought and 'make it real,' picturing the subject as holding this state of mind.

"After a few moments of meditation the leader would again say aloud, 'He cannot hurt the church: he has no power.'

"All would hold this sacred thought, concentrating and visualizing.

"The leader once more would continue: 'He is confused—he is confused.'

"Then all would picture the man in a state of mental confusion. If after such treatments, lasting sometimes half an hour a day for many months with the mental efforts of thirty people behind them, the victim did finally go insane, the outside world was allowed to understand that he was insane before he came into the church or he would never have defied Mrs. Stetson. Initiate members would be told that by the removal of the disobedient one God had protected his church.

"Actually, direct suggestion played a real and a large part in these 'treatments.' If the practitioners were treating a person with the object of 'confusing' him, giving him incapacitating disease, or rendering him unfit to conduct his business, word was allowed to reach the intended victim of the proceedings being followed. Those who already believed in the potency of mental power easily were impressed with the horror which was hanging over them.

It would not be strange if, in numerous instances after receiving such news of the practitioners' activities, members actually began to be sick and ailing.

"How the imagination of the more impressionable and hysterical members of the congregation was caught in a whirlpool of fear much like that in which Mrs. Eddy had engulfed herself may best be illustrated by the words of some of the sufferers. 'When I refused to yield my will to Mrs. Stetson,' one church member related, 'I aroused her enmity. One night as I lay in bed I felt that my hour had come, that mental forces which were almost irresistible were being directed against me. I called on God and for an hour I fought the fight. During that hour I developed such psychic faculties that I was able to make my body pass through the walls of my room. At last I conquered and have been safe since.'

"In cases where the practitioners thought themselves dealing with a particularly vicious enemy, the half-hour treatments were much extended: in the fashion Mrs. Eddy had established in years long past, a sort of guard mount was instituted, and the practitioners would take two-hour periods for the duty of holding it. One victim who had been told that he was being treated in this manner said that 'the strain of the malpractice on me was so great that to get peace of mind I rode in the noisiest cars and went into the noisiest parts of the city. I could hug the noise for the relief it gave me.'"*

My friends, there is ample evidence to show that Black Magic is not a matter to be treated lightly—"Fifty per cent. fraud and fifty per cent. bad observation," as our modern Kelvins might aver. No, it is a real influence, sometimes consciously and maliciously directed, but also, and for the main part, the result of fear, jealousy, lust, greed, and all the unpleasant emotions which the human heart can engender.

It is the fear of lack, and the greed for more than one's needs that has been the unseen Black Magic behind the slump, and the failure of the Economic Conference. What else could have caused a rich, self-supporting country like America to go into such depths of distress? America has enough of everything. People say, "Oh, but the system is wrong." Perhaps it is, but even when America was prosperous, her condition was alarming, because of gangsters and general immorality of all kinds. These things have a cause. They are not just an accident. A boy does not become a gangster without an unseen urge. The mental atmosphere becomes so thick with greedy thoughts, and with the vibrations of harsh money-getting, that receptive youths of a callow type, having no knowledge of "mind-tuning," simply get carried away. As with the gangster, so with the community: a vibration of thought, once

---

* From *Mrs. Eddy*, by Dakin.

started in the wrong direction, can not only ruin a character, but, if it be taken up by others, can bring an Empire down.

As I write these words the newspapers are full of an alleged plot on London and Paris by a foreign power. Stories are also going the rounds that so many of London's tube stations are being rebuilt because they will be needed in case of air attack. Millions of Frenchmen, Germans, Russians, and others are allowing thoughts of hatred and suspicion to darken their minds; not realizing that the very act of holding such thoughts is like harbouring and breeding disease germs. These evil, resentful and fearful thoughts are boiling up slowly and surely. Songs are being sung that breed hate (useless, needless, ridiculous hate), and these songs are, *in their effect*,* akin to the *mantrams* which we *Yogis* chant to attune ourselves to the universal vibrations of power. The *Yogis* chant good *mantrams*, but the peoples of the earth are chanting bad, war-ridden "mantrams" and are thereby putting themselves into tune with the Black Magic of hate and war.

The Bible, that great text-book of mental and spiritual power, contains some intriguing and interesting examples of the use of Black Magic. I am not presuming to judge the great characters of the Bible; but I think it is very noticeable that there was almost only one among them

---

* Notice carefully that I say "in their effect" for there is no other likeness between these opposite poles of Good and Evil.

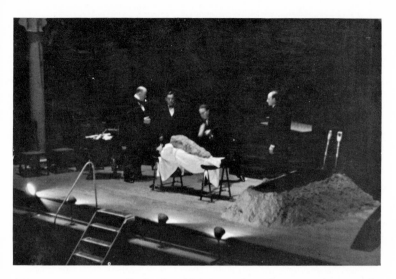

A huge stone rests on the body which is supported on two sharp scythe blades. The stone is broken by the heavy blows of a blacksmith's hammer.

PLATE I

A thick twelve-inch-long needle is pushed through the thigh by a member of the audience.

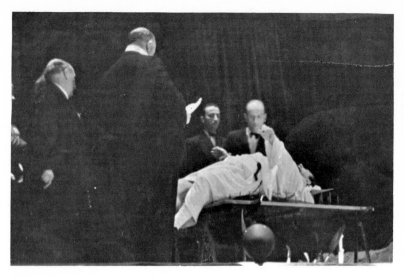

The unconscious body is laid on a bed of extremely sharp nails with unsterilized points.

PLATE II

A demonstration of a non-contact telepathy, the message having been written and sealed up by a member of the audience, quite unknown to anyone on the platform.

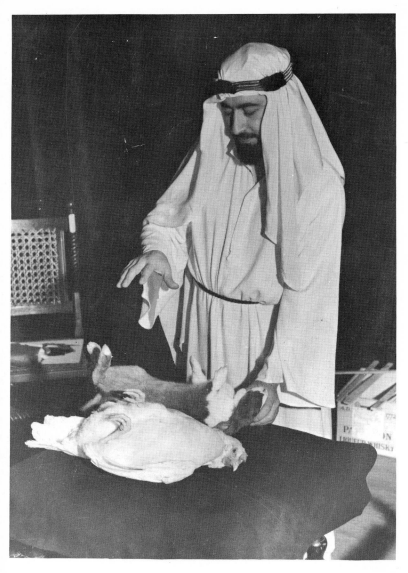

PLATE III

Physiological experiments on a hen and a rabbit, demonstrating the
preliminary stages through which the body passes in preparation for
the marvellous feat of burial.

PLATE IV

The Burial Scene. After the body is put in the coffin and covered with sand, the lid is firmly fixed and more sand is thrown on it.

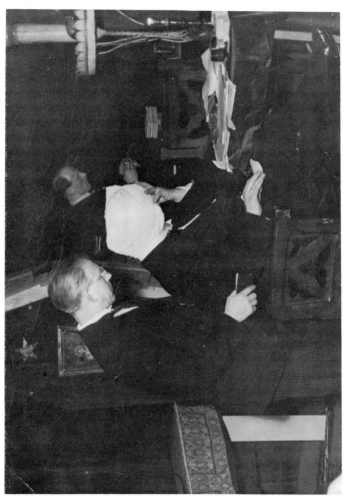

PLATE V

The Author uses his "Spiritual Sight".

By courtesy of "The Isle of Man Examiner"

Fire-eating. A two-foot wick, burning in paraffin oil, is allowed to fall into the mouth, and flames one to three feet high are then expelled.

PLATE VI

Another illustration of breaking a stone resting on the Yogi's body. The stone is too heavy for four men to lift. The Yogi lies on a bed of ten thousand nails. It is broken after many attempts, but the Yogi is uninjured.

Six heavy-weight members of the audience, standing on Kitao's body with a thin cloth only between them and him. His naked body is lying on the bed of ten thousand six-inch sharp nails (tested by spectators).

PLATE VII

Twelve strong spectators attempting to strangle Kitao with a strong rope tied in a slip-knot (examined by spectators).

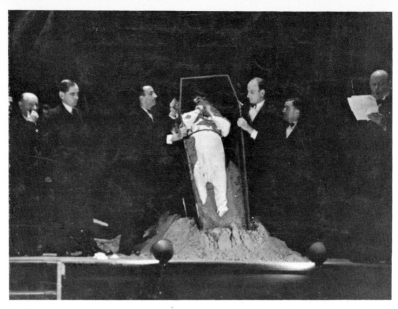

The return from the dead: once more the Fakir awakens, bringing back to life the great secrets of the Unknown from beyond the grave.

PLATE VII–A

Fourteen swords penetrate the "coffin" leaving no room for contortionist trickery.

Kitao's head being pierced by a three-foot sword penetrating it from above.

1.—HYPERTHYROID TYPE

2.—SUBTHYROID TYPE

3.—PITUITARY TYPE

4.—ADRENAL TYPE

5.—THYMUS CENTRED TYPE

6.—OVARIAN TYPE

PLATE VIII

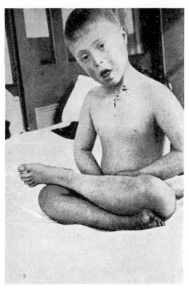

MONGOLIAN IDIOT
Note protuding tongue, and also the
Buddha attitude

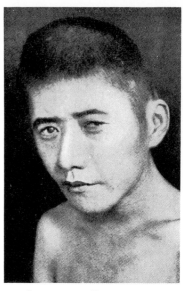

STIGMATA OF DEGENERATION
Note the misshaping of the head and
face (*see p.* 163)

CHONDRO-DYSTROPHIC DWARF—IDIOCY

MICROCEPHALIC IDIOT

PLATE IX

HYDROCEPHALIC IMBECILE
Note low position of ears as well as the size of the head

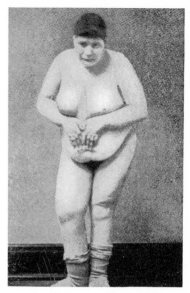

FRÖHLICH'S DISEASE
in a boy of 18 years
Adiposo-genital dystrophy

HÆMATOMA AURIS ("insane ear") and SYPHILITIC ALOPECIA AREATA (bald patches on head)

ACROMEGALY
in a woman of 38 years

PLATE X

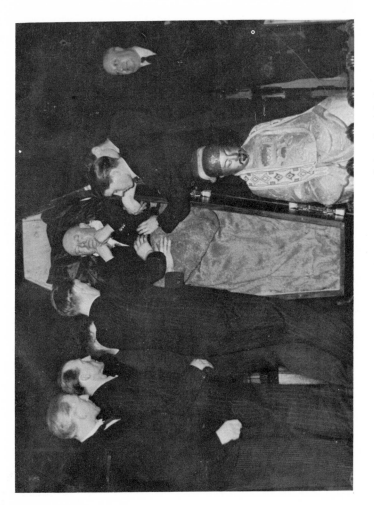

The Author gives a demonstration of the living burial.

who never used Black Magic: Jesus of Nazareth never used His power against others, but He once demonstrated its effect in the withering of a fig-tree. That He was tempted to do so, we are certain, for the story of the Temptation is undoubtedly the exoteric story of that great inner experience which comes to all men who tread *the Straight and Narrow Path*, and from that Temptation a man emerges either as a Black or a White Magician. Jesus, the greatest of all *Yogis*, conquered this temptation and He never allowed His power to be used wrongly or destructively. People sometimes say that the withering of the fig-tree, and the destruction of the Gadarene herd were examples of Black Magic; quite true, but these were merely demonstrations of its power.

Some of the Prophets whose histories are recorded in the Old Testament (and also St. Peter in the New Testament), used their power to destroy and to maim as well as to raise up and to heal. The slaying of the Egyptian first-born; the overthrowing of the Egyptian armies in the Red Sea; the slaughter of the priests of Baal; the infliction of leprosy and blindness: and the slaying of Annanias and Sapphira, all make rather distressing but enlightening reading. It is difficult for an orthodox Christian to pour moral scorn upon Communists, or Fascists because they kill their opponents, when the first Father of their own Church used his higher powers to protect the early Christian "Communists" by slaying Annanias and Sapphira. In truth these methods were very different from those of the gentle *Yogi* of Nazareth, who brought only blessing and peace to others and Himself suffered all the pain and the rejection. And, indeed, the meekness and the gentleness which men so marvel at in the Lord Jesus, and which has been mocked by shallow materialists, is the very quality which alone can dispel the evil vibrations of Black Magic.

On the pinnacle upon which He lived, the Christ was so sensitive to the vibrations of good and evil that He had to eschew all force and anger except the most righteous indignation. We cannot count evil and hatred false if we ourselves employ them and return evil for evil, and hatred for hatred. If we do not believe in the truth of these things, surely we ought not to dabble in them for our own soul's sake.

A favourite trick of Caruso's was to sing into a wineglass and break it; the glass would break because the vibrations of Caruso's voice were "sympathetic" to the "vibratory period" of the glass. So it is with you! If you allow yourself to become angry, or jealous, you will make your own mind vibrate in sympathy with the angry and jealous thought-vibrations in the world, and these will echo and re-echo upon your mind and claim you as their prey.

It is not enough for you to be merely negatively pure, just, and good: you must be positively pure, just, and good! A negative attitude of mind will allow strong evil influences to get into your mind. That is why so many people moan about their afflictions and say: "I never *thought* about evil; I never *thought* about disease: why should these things come to *me*?" My friends, it is not enough that you merely make your cups clean! You must also fill them with good wine: otherwise the Spirit of Evil will seize upon your clean cups and pour its evil potions thereinto—for "Nature abhors a vacuum" as much in the invisible world as it does in the visible world.

Evil must not be weakly avoided, but it must be thrown out with force. This is quite often seen where some evil influence is present— as in a haunted house. Often I have had people write to me saying that they are worried to death by unpleasant happenings in their houses. One letter comes by this morning's mail from a man who has read my book, THE INVISIBLE INFLUENCE, to ask my help in obtaining relief from a Poltergeist. It is not enough that these evil influences are neglected and ignored. They are real forces, and they must not be tampered with. The forces of faith must be brought to bear against them.

Did not Jesus say to His disciples when they came to Him and asked why they could not cast out devils: *If ye have faith as a grain of mustard seed, ye shall say unto this mountain, Remove hence to yonder place. . . . Howbeit this kind goeth not out but by prayer and fasting.* *

---

* Matthew, 17: 20-21.

This shows that spiritual power had to be exerted before the demons would respond to the command to go forth. They did not go out at a mere request. Evil is not to be overcome by namby-pambyism.

I wonder if it has ever struck anyone that the evil now in the world is very largely due to the conscious and unconscious Black Magic laid upon us by the past? Look at the Jews, for example. They are the remnant of the people whose great Prophets wrote the Bible, and who, being writers of a book of Life, must have been Adepts in their knowledge of Life. Do the Jews to-day realize what heavy curses were laid upon them by these men? Do they realize the terrible toll of Black Magic that is causing them so much misery? There are many passages in the Bible which state plainly that Israel and its Seed, if they contravene the Law, shall suffer grievous curses. Now, the Jews have broken some of the Law, and the Jews are being made the whipping-boys of the world. I speak not as an anti-Semite (how could I, preaching the power of Love, be guilty of such a foolish error?); but I speak as a friend of the Jews and of all men, and I say to the Jews that they are labouring under a curse laid upon them in days long since past, and I urge them to exorcize this spirit of evil, even though they are being saved from the full force of those curses because they, like the Egyptologists mentioned a few pages back, think that

Black Magic is impossible. I do not want to make the Jews believe in those curses until they also know how to exorcize them; but I want to encourage them to read their own Bible and see how many grievous curses are laid upon them. For they are the remnant of Israel and Israel was full of the knowledge of the power of Black and White Magic. The Prophets exhorted the people of Israel to avoid the "Evil Eye": *Eat thou not the bread of him that hath an evil eye . . . for as he thinketh in his heart, so is he.* *

As with the Jews, so it is with all the nations. What nation is there that has not been cursed by some dying enemy, or by some bitter foe? What man is there among us of whom somebody has not at some time held a vindictive and biting thought? Is there such a nation?— is there such a man? I doubt it. Therefore, knowing this, let us exorcize the evil thoughts which surround us. Let us daily pray to be delivered from this evil. Let us daily try to be more and more like children (pure in heart and willing to be guided) so that the evil may fade away because it can no more touch us than the Dragon in the fable could touch the innocent child who stood, clothed in the majesty of purity, before its very jaws.

As we do this we shall rise above the maelstrom: we shall behold life with purer eyes: we shall become superior to the tides and the winds of bitter fortune. We shall become

* Proverbs, 23:6-7.

masters of our own destiny, not in the sense of being mere freebooters (for there are no free men in the world at all); but we shall be enlisted in the ranks of Truth, and although we shall be men under authority (because, as I reiterate, none of us is free), we shall be enlisted in an army that must conquer in the end.

Before I close this lecture, I should like to give you two more examples of Black Magic which have come to my notice. The first of these is interesting, but permits of several possible explanations. The second will bring home to your innermost heart the terrible potency of this evil force, for it concerns the private life of a noble gentleman whose family tragedies have been much in the news during the past few years. Moreover, I want to bring my lecture to a fitting end by telepathic exorcism of the evil influence clinging about that nobleman's life.

The first story concerns the mother of a mental nurse. The lady is apparently quite sane, but she writes to me as follows:

"I saw visions of certain people at midnight, and I informed an aunt of mine who told me that if I would stick a knife through these visions they would trouble me no more.

"So after a time I saw a phantom of a person I knew, who lived across the road. It sailed into the room. I had a knife in my hand at the time, so I cut the phantom through.

"The next morning I was informed that Mrs.

X had died in a mysterious way the previous night, whilst sitting fully dressed in her chair.

"I never breathed a word to anyone, but a fortnight before Christmas the dead woman's daughter appeared just in the same way as a phantom and I cut through this phantom also. The girl died the same night without any illness."

These sudden deaths at the times stated have been confirmed, and the evidence appears quite correct. Two scientists and a lawyer investigated the case and found the details to tally with the woman's statement. Needless to say, action was taken to prevent recurrence, but, of course, nothing more specific may be published by me in this connection.

The second case of Black Magic, brings the terror of its power very near to us, for it concerns a Peer of the Realm of England. The statement given by a relative in a letter to me, reads as follows:

"While visiting Egypt with his wife in the spring, they entered the temple at Luxor for the purpose of seeing it as tourists. They found some kind of religious service in progress attended by a number of people, mostly Germans and Americans, with wreaths of roses on their heads, and reciting curious incantations and performing curious rites. Lord X and his wife moved about them looking at the temple. Their movements appeared to disturb the worshippers, one of whom requested the two visitors to leave the temple. His Lordship protested on the grounds that the temple was open to the public and that he and his wife had as much right of entrance as the worshippers, who, it appears, belong to a sect of Black Magicians . . . and were moreover worshippers of Isis to whom the Luxor temple is dedicated. The visitors took no notice of the request and continued to talk and move about. This annoyed the worshippers who again requested them to leave. His Lordship grew angry and a rather heated argument followed. Her ladyship became uneasy and thereafter left the temple, leaving her husband in the temple for he had become obstinate and was determined to remain there as long as he liked. He had with him a small ciné-camera, and appears to have tried to photograph some of the worshippers during their rites. This so infuriated them that their priest interrupted the service and advancing upon his Lordship solemnly cursed him and the whole of his family.

"The following December his second son was killed in a street accident and the following July his wife was killed in an air disaster. Three weeks previously his little nephew died during an operation. The next year his father died, and there has been scarcely a member of the family who has not been afflicted by either illness or death. His Lordship has since tried to get into touch with the sect in order to make his peace and ask for the removal of the curse, but the

worshippers have since scattered over the wide
world, never to re-unite in Egypt, leaving no
trace, and he has been unsuccessful. It has also
been established since that the sect had no
right whatever to worship in that or any other
of the Egyptian temples, as the strict law of the
Egyptian Government is that no service of any
kind may be held in any of the temples."

The writer of this pathetic letter begged me
to help, and I am happy to comply with that
request. The curse *shall* be removed. A
petition to God never fails, for it is written:
*Whatsoever ye ask the Father in My name, He will
give unto you.* *

To the Black Magician who cursed this nobleman in that Luxor Temple, I solemnly telepathize the following words of Isaiah:

> *My Word shall not return unto me void,
> but shall accomplish that whereunto it is
> sent.†*

And I, therefore, send forth these further
words to that Black Magician:

> *Thy word shall also return unto thee,
> and the curse which thou hast placed upon
> the head of this our most noble and respected
> lord, now returns to thee and lies upon
> thine own head and upon thine own house!
> Curses, like chickens, come home to roost.*

---

* John 14:13.   † Job, 22: 25.

THE EVIDENCE OF POWER
(The Magic-Lantern of the Mind)

(The following chapter is based upon three talks: one given at the Annual Dinner of the British College of Psychic Science held at the Café Royal on Wednesday, May 9th, 1934, another given at the Grotian Hall on July 2nd, 1934, and a third delivered at the Spa Theatre, Bridlington, January 27th, 1934.)

Jesus Christ, the great Nazarene Yogi, said quite clearly that people whose minds were closed to spiritual powers would not believe though one rose from the dead. Yet visual evidence may be necessary to some types of minds, and it is to these minds, in part, that this chapter is directed—though, indeed, there will be many more who, whilst they have faith that spiritual power is a reality, will be thrilled by the added evidence in support of their faith.

These minds that doubt are not to be criticized. They stand at the point of evolution where the cross roads once again demand a choice. It is a serious matter for them and it demands of them every ounce of their knowledge and faith. Like Thomas, they must have just that little extra guarantee of the reality of the territory into which they are bidden to enter, before they can become real settlers in the new evolutionary world.

In the pages that follow it will be the author's great privilege and pleasure to state a few of the miracles of mind-body control which he has witnessed in the Far East. Miracles we call them—or magic. But they are only miracles to us in the same way that our speech is a miracle to a dog: or would be if he could comprehend that speech exists. To more highly evolved beings the things described here are commonplace matters. The world is an illusion and can be dealt with as such.

May the evidence of the following pages help to impress the minds of those labouring souls who are just at the point where they would fain believe and are yet tormented by doubt.

CHAPTER SIX

THE essence of psychic power is the control by mental means of that which we are used to calling matter. To those who live engrossed in the toils of matter it is nonsense to suppose that there is any escape from matter until death sets us free. Yet the *Yogi* knows full well, as I have already made known to you, that there is no such thing as a "solid" world in which we are captives of our bodies. We are captives only so long as we choose to stay captives, and all the religion of the world, if it were only understood, would be seen to be the urge in the hearts and minds of humanity to set us free from these limitations of matter. The human race is nearing the point where the world it has known for so many centuries is nearing its end. The end is fast approaching amid the alarms of war and the cataclysms of nature. But the end will be more glorious than its approach, for the day dawns when men will be freed of limitation if they will only stand up and claim their birthright.

Therefore, lift up your hearts and your minds

and master your desires, for your desires are the snare in which limitation holds you. The desire is the bait in the trap of matter. It is the lure that ends in the snare of the fowler. Control yourself and you will be set free. Did not Jesus, the greatest *Yogi* of all time, say to His disciples that if they were faithful in a little they should be made rulers over many things. Control of desire is the key to the problem of control of nature.

Come, now, with me in spirit to the mysterious and but newly opened land of the East, where men have learned to control their desires and have, as a result, been given control of the external world in which they live and move and have their being. Let your mind travel with me as I describe to you scenes which have actually met my enquiring eye as I made my pilgrimage into the Far East. Remember that I did not go to be deceived, and if the story I relate to you seems to your Western ears a fantastic one, just remind yourself that my eyes are the trained eyes of a scientist and not the bemused eyes of a poet. Remember that nothing should be taken for granted, and that Lord Lister, the great bacteriologist, was laughed to scorn by the doctors of his day because he said that gangrenous or septic wounds were the result of living organisms. Yet for thousands of years the great knowledge of the East has existed which makes even Lord Lister's work seem very small: for this knowledge tells us that we may control the growth of microscopic organisms by mental means, and may say to the wounded man: "Your wounds shall not become gangrenous: there shall be no sepsis," and it shall be as we command it. I have put a man into an hypnotic sleep in the Mayfair Hotel before a great crowd of doctors and laymen, and I have run a large tie-pin through his ear.* The man felt nothing at all, but one anxious doctor, peering at the patient, asked me if the needle were sterilized. To my answer that it was not sterilized, he urged me to tell him why I was not afraid of blood-poison. "Because the patient is under my control," I answered him. "Likewise the whole of his organism is under my control. Every blood cell; every micro-organism. If I tell him that there will be no sepsis, then that message will go down to the very depths of his being and in those unseen depths, where all the delicate action of his body is controlled, the command will be uttered in resounding terms: THERE CAN BE NO SEPSIS." Then I leaned over the sleeping man whose ear was punctured by the pin, and I said to him in a commanding tone, "THERE CAN BE NO SEPSIS!"

But, come, we are wasting time trying to convince you that there is a reason for the faith that is in us. Surely this book is full of

---

* Upon the occasion of the First Mayfair Tea-Talk at which I assisted my very dear friend the late Professor Alexander Erskine, the world-famous hypnologist.

reason and may now permit of a little straight-forward recital of facts. You are with me now in that land of light and snow, in the extreme North-East of Thibet, where we shall find the Kum Bum Monastery at Amod near the Great Blue Lake.

Do you see that man with the grave, saintly face and the luminous eyes? He is bending over a small bird that has fallen dead with cold in the snows which surround the monastery; for remember that we are now at a height of 10,700 feet above sea level, and 500 miles north-east of Lhasa the temporal capital of Thibet, and 500 miles West of the nearest Chinese railroad.

What is he going to do? He picks up a lens such as we have here in the West, for they have quite modern lenses there, and he concentrates the light of the sun into each of the bird's eyes for fifteen seconds at a time. He is a *Yogi* who is practised in the Solar Science, and one who knows a great deal about the connections between the different vibrations of light, music, thought, and even life itself. See how the little bird in his hand suddenly begins to manifest signs of life! Look! It is actually hopping about the ground. Now it attempts to fly! It actually flies, and hops with delight from twig to twig.

Let us pass on together to a change of scene. That man over there is a lhama who lives and works at this great monastery. As we approach him he simply vanishes into thin air. He's gone! We now walk up to where he was, just to satisfy ourselves that he is not there, when we feel something thrust us aside and, behold, he appears once more to us and is standing visible in our midst. How great a marvel can he reveal to us? How childlike is all our vaunted Western knowledge?

Once again the scene changes. We are now in the presence of the Grand Lhama of the Kum Bum Monastery—the lamaserie of a thousand images. The Lhama chants in melodious tones, which resemble the slow chimes of Big Ben played on a 'cello, until we can literally see colours surrounding him, produced as it were by the reaction of his chanting upon a very much finer essence than the air which carries his voice to us. He seems, indeed, to touch some chord of light, power and of peace which passeth all understanding.*

Now three wise men approach us and ask us for our commands. The Grand Lhama (not the Great Lhama of Lhasa be it understood) warns us not to touch them, for they are but shadows. Even as he speaks, the seeming wise men vanish in the twinkling of an eye, and we learn that they are the visions of three men who were in a state of trance at the time we spoke

---

* Here followed a demonstration of the effect of sound waves produced by slow music. A gramophone record of "Rose Mousse," Columbia DB746, was played at a speed of 68 instead of 78 as recommended by the makers. The result was astounding, and the experiment should be tried by the reader. He will be astounded at the rest and the peace which comes to him from the pulsing notes of this slow music. He should sit with closed eyes, relaxed body, and he should breathe in measured rhythm.

with them. To be exact, they were lying in a trance at a little village called Sido situated some miles south of the monastery of Kum Bum, and when we visit them there we find that they had indeed spoken with us and heard our commands which they had obeyed to the minutest detail.

Come back with me now to England, that dear land of dread common sense and stubbornness. Allow me to present to you the exact copy of a letter which I have written to the Editor of the BRITISH MEDICAL JOURNAL concerning the statements of Colonel Elliot in regard to the Indian Rope Trick. For I can claim to have seen this trick performed: or, rather, I should say that it is no trick at all, but a feat of collective hypnosis. The trick does not take place. What happens is that a Fakir impresses the mark of his own vivid imagination so strongly upon the surrounding sea of mental ether that every person who enters that sphere of influence is at once affected by it. There is no reason why the "trick" thus imposed upon the minds of the "observers" should consist of the Rope Trick. Any unusual or impossible phenomenon can be rendered "visible." I know of people who have had the desert peopled with crows by a Fakir until the whole surrounding country was thick with them. Do you not see that what they are doing is to control the *Maya* about them so that, in turn, they are shaping your world for you? The world for a certain space of time, and over a certain area, appears to run

contrary to the normal procedure of law. Once
you have grasped the idea at the back of the
Yoga philosophy you will not be puzzled by
such "miracles," but you will instead be
utterly amazed to think that the West can have
remained so long in ignorance of these things,
particularly when they are a part of the orthodox belief of Western nations. Of course, the
explanation is that the West has got over the
difficulty by explaining that Christianity is
based upon the life of a God and not upon the
life of the greatest *Yogi* of all time.

The West is ready enough to spend its money
in going to see conjuring tricks, and will flock
to see Mr. Maskelyne's marvels. But it will not
see that these things are but a pale shade of the
real marvels which do not depend upon sleight
of hand nor upon the deception of the eye. It
cannot see that human beings are indeed
endowed with power to shape life to their
own ends. That power and happiness and all
the necessities of life can be ours if we will. It
cannot see that the Indian Rope Trick* is not a
parlour trick designed to amuse small minds for
an hour, but that the only merit in discussing
it at all lies in the fact that it is a splendid bit
of evidence of the powers which lie in all men.
What one *Yogi* can do, all men may do if they
devote themselves to following the Path.
Many are called, but few are chosen, said the

---

* I do not refer to the conjurers' tricks with specially prepared
ropes or the bamboo pole.

great Jesus Christ, but He also pointed out that those who followed Him would be able to do the works that He did and greater works even than His.

We shall never understand what this means to us if we believe that Nature is a solid condition of life which we are powerless to alter. We shall then take childish delight in conjuring-tricks and delude ourselves that nothing greater can be achieved.

This is precisely the impasse into which the Magic Circle has been led by its own misconceptions. One cannot blame it. Its members are only being used as focusing-points for the generality of Western thought. What they think is being hypnotized upon them by the materialistic ethic of the West held in the minds of millions of thinking men and women, whose thought has not reached a level at which these greater things can be accepted.

So the Magic Circle demands to see the Indian Rope Trick, not understanding that it will never see it as it desires to see it, but that it will be made to see it with the eyes of a self-hypnotized man.

Here is my letter on the subject:

LONDON, 27TH FEBRUARY, 1934

TO THE EDITOR,

"BRITISH MEDICAL JOURNAL," LONDON.

Sir,

I have read Colonel Elliot's letter on Collective Suggestibility concerning the Indian Rope Trick.

May I draw the Colonel's attention to THE INVISIBLE INFLUENCE where I distinctly state that the Indian Rope Trick is a visual hallucination and I give adequate evidence in support of my statement. I have seen the "rope trick" performed in the presence of Monsieur Robert of the French Consulate in Indo-China. Let me describe what we saw.

The scene is a palm-shaded Eastern market-place. In the centre thereof stands the Ascetic. His eyes half open, he stands waving his arms, gesticulating, and uttering *Yogi* incantations, meanwhile swaying gently to the rhythm. In front of him is a coiled red-coloured rope lying upon the ground. Over this he stretches out his hands periodically. On his right hand side stands a youth who has a most noticeable far-away dreamy expression in his eyes. The *Yogi* (of this lowest sixth class of the *Yoga* philosophy), carefully preserves a semi-circle at a suitable distance of twelve feet radius as the crowd draws near, ever surging and ever swelling. At last the Ascetic stoops, and lifts up the end of the red rope, and holds it out at arm's length. The end of the rope then appears to rise higher and higher, as if drawn heaven-wards by an invisible force, and this process continues until the other end of the rope is just free of the ground. The *Yogi* then motions the boy to take hold of the rope, and to climb. This the youth does, reaching first the upper end of the rope, remaining with it in mid-air. Then he comes down to the ground once more by climbing down the rope. The Real *Yogi* does not stop here. The boy again climbs the rope and the *Yogi* appears to follow him up the rope with a knife clenched in his teeth. He gets hold of the boy, cuts him to pieces, and appears to drop the different parts of the body to the ground, where they lie quivering in the dust. The magician then descends the rope, puts the pieces of the body together and then sends the youth up to the top of the rope again, and when he reaches the top, the boy and the rope appear to vanish into thin air.

As regards evidence of even greater things than those may I refer Colonel Elliot to the following:

Sir Ernest Wallis Budge writes in THE DAILY EXPRESS of January the 17th, 1934. "I knew an African and an Indian who could vanish into air as you spoke to them. Like the Cheshire cat in ALICE IN WONDERLAND, first they were there, then there was only the grin, then that too, disappeared. It was no question of hypnotism* for I walked through the spot where they had been standing. In the same way they would re-appear and as they solidified, pushed me away.

"One of them could even materialize my subordinates who were twenty miles away,

_____
* As understood in the West.

within twenty yards of my eyes. These
materializations spoke to me and took my
orders. I was warned not to touch them,
because they were only shadows. But when I
arrived at the place where they were actually
working, I found my orders had always been
carried out. The men had heard them in a
trance. . . . Etc., etc.''

I am sure Sir Ernest Wallis Budge could help
the Occult Committee of the Magic Circle.

In the January number of THE WORLD WIDE
MAGAZINE there was an article on '' WIZARDRY
IN ALGERIA,'' where confirmatory evidence is
forthcoming from Government departments.
Allow me just to cite one incident.

''An even more amazing incident actually
involved the famous Surêté in Paris.

''In the centre of the desolate area between
Le Kreider and Bedeau lies the little village of
Marhoum. During the spring of 1929 Medicine
Capitaine Dubois was residing here, fighting
a diphtheria epidemic. He was a perfect sceptic
and was one day told of a certain shepherd
named Abdul Ouab who was possessed of
supernatural powers. Dubois is a famous
toxicologist, also.

''For his amusement when he had cleared up
the epidemic, Abdul Ouab was summoned and
asked to perform the 'tricks.'

''He told the captain Dubois to think of
some object in his palatial house in Paris which
he would like to see. Dubois concentrated his

mind on a very valuable family portrait valued at close on a quarter of a million francs.

"'*Look behind you*,' said Abdul Ouab. There on the wall hung the portrait. ' *Mon Capitaine*,' continued the shepherd, '*you may do just what you like with the picture during the day, but it must be returned to Paris by sunset.*'

"So saying, the Arab went back to mind his sheep.

"Unable to accept the evidence of his eyes and his hands, Dubois sent for the District Commissioner, the Postmaster and the Hospital Sergeant. Each of them not only saw but *handled* the picture.

"At the suggestion of the Commissioner a cable was sent 'Express Official' to Dubois' parents in Paris. At midday he received the following reply: *Portrait inexplicably stolen this morning. Police at work and Sûreté announces arrest of thief imminent.* *

"Shortly before sunset Abdul Ouab returned and politely enquired whether the Captain had finished with the picture. The Arab then made a gesture and the portrait vanished. Some hours later Dubois received a second telegram from his father: *Portrait returned as inexplicably as it vanished. Two Sûreté inspectors present in room and saw it appear on wall. Mother completely unnerved.*

"Captain Dubois is no longer a perfect sceptic. If you doubt this story write to Captain J. B.

---

* The Sûreté is the " Scotland Yard " of France.

Norton, of Timimoun, Algeria, and to M. Jean Lamoine, c/o Barclays Bank (France) Ltd., Lyons."*

Major Pogson of the Indian Army and Water Diviner to the Government of Bombay, writes to me on 16th December, 1933, as follows:

"I think it was in May, 1925, when wandering along the banks of the Nerbudda River that I happened upon one who had renounced the world and given himself up to the study of higher plane matters. Seated on a chaoa,† playing a certain instrument and repeating the 'constant' word, I must admit he presented a unique picture. This caused my companion to inspect him from various angles, pass some remarks in English not altogether complimentary, and eventually to exclaim, *I wonder if he would mind if I took his photo?* The reply came in perfect English that he would not have the slightest objection, providing some prints were sent to him for presentation to his chelas. I offered apologies explaining my companion did not realize that he would understand English. He replied that he would equally well have understood had the remarks been in any language. As far as I could test him, this assertion appeared to be true. In the course of a long conversation we happened to touch on the subject of conscious projection of self. His

---

*These gentlemen travel far and wide, and therefore replies to letters may be much delayed.

† A Yogi's mat.

parting words to me were, *Do not forget to send me the prints—if the matter is forgotten, I will be with you on your August 10th, where-ever you may be.* I wandered on to other places and the incident passed from my mind until one day in my office while engaged upon compiling a report and deep in my work, I saw before me on the paper in miniature the scene when he had uttered his parting words. I recalled his admonition and turning round looked at the calendar when I observed that it *was* August 10th. A point that struck me was that I had made a mistake in the date that morning as when I looked at my report I saw I had put the 9th."

These records go on *ad infinitum*: therefore to the Occult Committee of the Magic Circle I would address this modified Shakespearean saying: "There are more things in Heaven, (in Hell), and on Earth than ever we dreamt of." If you know where to look for the evidence you will find it!

I am, etc.,

ALEXANDER CANNON.

Since writing the above letter I have entered into communication with the Magic Circle, only to find that they were prepared to offer £500 for the performance of the "trick." This in itself, as you will see by now, is the result of a complete misunderstanding of the nature of the "trick." The people who made the offer probably thought that a half-dressed Indian would be brought from his distant forests, placed upon a stage and asked to display his powers. What they do not understand is that certain conditions are necessary for the trick to be performed: actual physical conditions which govern the condition of the people who are to be mass hypnotized. As I shall tell you in a later lecture, certain conditions of light and temperature are necessary to render a person right for hypnotizing. How important the existence of proper lighting is may be judged from the fact that I have invented a little instrument which enables a person to be hypnotized by light alone.* Some hospitals on the Continent actually use hypnosis by light for the treatment of certain cases. If light is so important in the hypnosis of *one* person, can you not readily see how terribly important it would be in the attempt to mass-hypnotize thousands? If you put a *Yogi* on the stage of the Albert Hall and asked him to display his powers, do you suppose he could do in the cold grey lighting of that building what he could do in the hypnotic light of the Indian setting sun? Do not forget that it is the *minds* of the audience that have to be affected—not their *eyes*. You can no more give a satisfactory display of the Indian Rope Trick in the wrong atmosphere than you could give a satisfactory dancing display in complete darkness. Light is needed

* The Cannon Hypnoscope—see page 155.

to enable the eyes to be affected by the vibrations from the bodies of the dancers: in the same way, proper mental and physical conditions are necessary to enable the minds of an audience to be affected by the vibrations from the mind of a Fakir performing the Rope Trick.

There are doubtless bound to be those folk who jump to the conclusion that because special conditions are necessary for the performance of the Indian Rope Trick, the whole thing must be a sham and an illusion. An illusion it most certainly is; but it is not by any means a sham. And since we are speaking of illusion again, does it not strike you what a wonderful achievement it would be if we understood more about illusion. After reading this book, can you not see to what an incredible extent "illusion" controls your destiny, your health, and your pocket. Does it not strike you that we shall be able to empty our hospitals, and our lunatic asylums, and our poor-houses, and our battlefields once we understand the basic nature of the "mind-stuff" (or "illusion-stuff") of which our visible universe is built. Can you not see what is in store for humanity when it accepts the grand facts before it. I am sure you can see that by now, and I am sure that you are not in need of much more evidence of these Powers That Be.

But in case you should still have a lingering fear in your minds that there must be a catch in it somewhere if the *Yogi* has to stay in India or Thibet to enable him to do the things claimed for him, let me assure you that *Yogis* have been here and have performed these so-called miracles. They have given examples of their powers in the presence of hundreds of doctors: their powers have been studied by the Western scientists. Why, then, have we made no sensational change in the outlook of the West? Simply because the ethic of the West is a materialistic one, and into the framework of that ethic the things of the mind and the spirit simply do not fit—at least, not until they are distorted out of all shape and mangled out of all semblance to reality.

Let me tell you about a friend of mine, Doctor Tahra Bey, who came to this country at my telepathic instigation in 1926* and gave an example of his powers before a large gathering of doctors held at the Scala Theatre. Tahra Bey did not have to mass-hypnotize the doctors as the performers of the Rope Trick would have to do. Therefore, he could work in the cold light of day or rather, under the cold combined glare of the Scala Theatre footlights, and of a lot of English doctors. You can read the report of this demonstration at the end of this chapter where there is reprinted a report made for THE SPECTATOR by Major Yeats-Brown, the distinguished author of BENGAL LANCER.†

I first met Doctor Tahra Bey in Le Touquet

---

* I was at this time in the mystic Orient.
† Appendix, *A Path to Peace*, by F. Yeats-Brown.

some years ago, when I attended a demonstration given by him in a hall attached to the Casino. I entered the hall with a friend, expecting to see a sort of glorified Maskelyne show. I may say that I had not then fully learned the mysteries of the mind and the spirit, and was deeply absorbed in the intricacies of Western science, the premises of which had not then been seriously questioned by me. We had not long to wait before there entered upon us a tallish dark man wearing a white head-dress and walking with an unhurried but deliberate mien. Those of us who possessed the slightest perception were not long in realizing that we were not in the presence of a showman. This Tahra Bey, olive-skinned, black-bearded, his face bearing an expression of deep serenity, his penetrating eyes soft with an Oriental wistfulness, seemed to radiate waves of mysterious influence and of remarkable potency. A showman indeed! Tahra Bey might have been a Hebrew prophet stepped straight from the pages of the family Bible.

An operating-table was brought on to the raised platform and Tahra Bey was laid thereon. He was stripped bare to the waist, and a huge stone was place on his abdomen and broken to bits by a large hammer. After a brief rest, his arms, face, neck, and legs were cut and pierced with pins, knives and small bits of glass. A knife was plunged into his chest and withdrawn, whereafter he caused the blood to flow and to cease flowing at will. The wound quickly healed,* and his pulse was tested. It was shown that he had complete control of his pulse, for he could make it beat fast or slow at will. He then carried out a series of telepathy tests with those members of the audience who would volunteer to help him. Gripping the wrists of the volunteer, he would ask him to concentrate upon the thought of some object on the person of a friend in the room. For a time he would look piercingly into the eyes of the volunteer, then suddenly without any warning he would turn to the one upon whose person the article was carried and demand its production. Never once did he fail to find the article of which the volunteer was thinking.

All this was quite astounding enough, but more was yet to come. At the end of this display Tahra Bey allowed himself to be buried in such a way that his breathing was entirely suspended. Practically all such demonstrations by him are done whilst he is in a state of auto-catalepsy. This is the secret of his ability to endure treatment that would otherwise involve tremendous and atrocious pain. To induce auto-catalepsy he arrests the vital functions, such as respiration and circulation, in such a manner that the sensitive nerve-centres are numbed as if by an anæsthetic.

This catalepsy is induced as follows. First the fingers are pressed upon the neck-arteries

---

* Within ten minutes to his own command.

and upon the hypnotic centres of the temples. Next the body is lightly balanced whilst the mind is concentrated upon the idea of loss of consciousness. Thirdly, the tongue is swallowed and air is brusquely inhaled.

When, on the particular evening in question, Tahra Bey carried out these processes, he fell back rigid, as if dead, into the arms of an assistant. Examination revealed no evidence of breathing or heart-beats. His body was then laid in a coffin, his nostrils were stuffed with cotton-wool, and several guests helped to pile the coffin high with sand. The lid was then placed in position, and a pyramid of sand was built up over it. For an hour we were left in suspense, to amuse ourselves as best we could. After that time the sand was swept aside, the lid removed, and Tahra Bey was taken out and placed in an arm-chair.

His face was absolutely ashen, and it seemed that he must be dead. But there appeared gradual signs of life, and after about fifteen minutes the Fakir was sitting up and telling us a few of the more superficial facts concerning his powers.

Among other things, he told us that long ago in ancient Egypt such feats were practised quite commonly, and it was found that the enforced repose which the organism was made to endure was a salutary remedy for many diseases. The practice, however, tends to shorten the life of the Fakir, and it is said that one year of such forced repose results in a shortening of the life by about two years. Tahra Bey, however, is not interested in this feat as a mere "stunt," but believes that whilst the body is wasting away under the earth, the mind is growing. He has since, I understand, decided to go to Egypt for a prolonged period of such rest. In the small booklet written by him on the subject, I read that he was so buried for one month whilst in Greece in 1923. In Rome the police would not allow a period longer than half an hour. At the time of the demonstration which I witnessed Tahra Bey was thirty years of age. He stated then that he was willing to lose three years of his life in this manner for purely scientific reasons. "If I were to wait," he explained, "it would be too late, for when the first youth has passed away a man's body cannot endure the prolonged inertia."

Here I would like to state that the training of a Fakir begins at a very early age. He begins to be trained at the age of three months and his psychic power is therefore extremely strong. His training consists of acquiring a remarkable insensitivity to wounds, of throwing himself into a state of catalepsy, of stopping his breathing, reading and controlling thoughts, and generally developing his powers over the processes of life and manifestation. In his desire to know the truth of the Eternal Enigma, the Fakir descends as far as possible into the abyss of death so that he may sound it as one sounds a well with a plummet. He simulates physical death so nearly by means of the profound lethargy which he induces, that he actually places himself at the point where decomposition of the body begins.

One thing we noticed very definitely after the last demonstration had been given by Tahra Bey, and that was the complete absence of scars on the Fakir's body, although he had been badly cut about and punctured with various weapons. The explanation given by him of this remarkable fact is interesting. Three things, he says, are necessary to the avoidance of scars. The first of these is a heightening of the pulse rate from the usual 60 to 70 beats a minute to about 120 to 135 a minute. The second is the temperature, and the third is the control of the micro-organisms which usually breed in a wound. No one of these conditions alone will have the desired effect, but the three things together will heal the wound in a remarkably short space of time.

My friend, the powers that lie undeveloped in your own mind and heart are not less than those manifested by this great man. Can you not see that the whole world is going into ruin because men are contending for their little desires instead of looking forward with open eyes and parted lips to the great world of power in which we live. For them the whole of life is a dog-fight for three-score years and ten in a three-dimensional world of matter. They do not see that Time and Space do not affect the realities of Life for those who have ears to hear and eyes to see. Therefore, do not cast my words aside and disbelieve what I say simply because I tell you of things foreign to your mind. Be as a little child! Open your eyes and your mind! Let these "foreign" things become real to you! Remember that what I have described to you is known to the doctors of the world and to the scientific men as well, but that it needs your help, and your acceptance, and your faith, to enable it to become accepted on a world-wide scale and so lift the shackles from man.

Doctor Tahra Bey himself worked in Rome before the Government and the whole Diplomatic Corps. Mussolini received him many times at the Chigi Palace, and learnt many secrets from him. King Victor Emmanuel commanded his presence. King George the Fifth of England, who was at Palermo during the Fakir's visit to that city, also expressed a desire to see his work.

Yet the world has gone blindly on its way; and war, dissolution, pain, and death seem more imminent every day.

Do not think that I do not know the doubts and fears which assail your mind as you ponder upon my exhortation. I myself once believed unquestioningly in the materialist theories of the West. I have had to meet every objection

point by point, step by step. It was this un-
expected visit of Doctor Tahra Bey to Paris
Plage and Le Touquet that again lifted me high
enough to enable me to see the possibilities of
developing and sensitizing the "tentacles" of
the human organism (comprising the spiritual
as well as the "material" attributes of man) so
that it might be able to contact with new knowledge outside the reach of the human brain.
Do not think that I despise the brain. No one
may despise what God has created. But though
the brain may be an exquisite instrument, like
the "brain" of a Newton or a Kepler, it can never
in itself rest upon eternal verities, for it is all
the time advancing in a different direction. The
intellect is always advancing laterally, along the
levels of Time and Space, whereas spiritual
comprehension soars upward. It is, as it were,
a new faculty, sometimes completely opposed
in its findings to the brain which seems to lead
up to it. Have we not all known men and
women who have become more and more perfect in their reasoning powers, but who have
been led by this very perfection farther and
farther from any knowledge of spiritual truth.
To-day in the West we cannot fail to notice a
sad atrophying of the spiritual faculty in favour
of the purely intellectual and mechanical.

But this process can only go on until it kills
itself. The plant that has withdrawn its roots
from the gentle earth can only die. Even so is
this Age dying: its material basis is producing

horrors that will turn upon it and rend it. But with its disappearance, though it be by a peaceful death or a violent one, will come the resurgence of Life, and that resurgence will be based upon the increasing knowledge of the powers which I have verbally demonstrated to you in this chapter.

For the things of which I have told you are indeed true. They indicate that the "miracles" of the New Testament, and of the Old Testament too, are not a fiction. They indicate that a power lies in our hearts that is greater than all the powers of exploding gases and expanding steam by which we place such store and upon which our civilization is built.

For in our hearts and minds there is the power to mould Earth into the pattern of God's Kingdom. Every great religious leader has spoken of that power. Christ Himself spoke of it in no uncertain terms. Seek for it! Live it! So that you (and all around you by the force of your example) will step by step reveal your unseen talents and become a super-personality, dominated by the power of Universal Love.

APPENDIX

A PATH TO PEACE

Reprinted from THE SPECTATOR of May 29th, 1926 by kind permission of the Editor.

The "Egyptian fakir," Dr. Tahra Bey, gave rather a ghastly show of his powers to some doctors and journalists recently. But I think the attitude of a part of the audience was more unpleasant than anything the fakir showed us.

When he drove a knife through the skin of his throat, or when an eminent surgeon put a bodkin (that may not be the medical name, but it looked like a bodkin) right through the fakir's forearm, women turned away in horror and one of them fainted. A journalist near by me said it was "disgusting," and went out to have a drink at the expense of the management. Why did these people come to see experiments, whose object it is to prove that pain is an illusion, if they are so mentally enmeshed in illusion and if their imagination is so uncontrolled that they sicken at the sight of the illusion of suffering? Part of the audience made me ashamed of Western civilization, with its physical puerilities and mental arrogance. At the same time, there is no doubt that the performance is unsuitable for the public stage. The public would neither appreciate it nor understand it; indeed, it would do nothing but feed the sadistic instincts of what I hope is a minority.

And yet Dr. Tahra Bey has a real message to give to the West. If he only convinced half a dozen of the hundred doctors present at the *séance* his work may have good results. New ideas of value to mankind rarely come to us panoplied and fully armed, ready to fend for themselves in the world. Our doctors will have to clothe and equip this three-thousand-year-old physiological psychology of the East with their own scientific formulæ.

There is no doubt in my mind that Dr. Tahra Bey is of the order of those Aryan Melchizedeks who evolved the various systems of Yoga. Technically he is a Sufi, I suppose, but spiritually he follows a branch (*Gathasthayog*) of that lofty philosophy of the Vedas of whose teachings Max Muller, Schopenhauer and Swedenborg said that their dissemination would one day produce a spiritual Renaissance in Europe. As a student of these subjects for twenty years, as a disciple moreover along similar but less professional lines than the fakir's, I can affirm that there is nothing either in Yoga in general or in the Sufi doctrine in particular that need disturb the faith or injure the mental balance of any Western inquirer. On the contrary, control of breath and nerve-reactions will bring peace where no peace was, and new energy to slaves of wrong thought and wrong nutrition. Here, in Dr. Tahra Bey, is a Christian Scientist *in excelsis*. He says there is no pain (*"La douleur est une opinion"*). He sticks two skewers through his tongue and another through both cheeks, offers to let the doctors cut him about as they will, and when the knife-blade enters his flesh, his pulse registers not a throb the more. But at will he can accelerate his heart beats. These things he does beyond shadow of doubt. Whether it be true that he can heal his wounds by speeding up his circulation I do not know.

"You don't feel pain if you don't think about it," said the fakir in his soft but very audible French. "Yesterday I saw a little girl who had fallen down and scratched her arm. She didn't stop playing but went on running about, so that her abrasions healed quickly. I do the same with my wounds. My body really belongs to me—all of it heart, digestive tract, nerves. I can repair any damage in my tissues. I can also slow down my pulse and go into a profound and restful slumber, which indeed is more like hibernation than sleep."

No doubt doctors will say that in cases of hysteria they

have seen a similar anæsthesia. But have they ever seen control such as Dr. Tahra Bey's? I observed him very carefully, comparing him with teachers I have worked with in India and elsewhere. The fakir had the same powerful neck, the same deep lungs, the same poised rhythm of walk, the same level eyes as the Brahmins of the Ganges side, our Aryan cousins of a remote antiquity.

There is no particular mystery about anything that the fakir does. He claims only to have educated his ego, so that he has obtained full domination over the physical body and over his states of mind. In half a minute he can throw himself into a trance. After some invisible breathing exercises he presses the pneumo-gastric nerves on each side of his neck, turns the tip of his tongue back into his throat and becomes "dead to the world." In this state he can be buried alive for periods up to six hours. This experiment was demonstrated to us at the Scala the other night for ten minutes. Now ten minutes is longer than a man of even abnormal lung power can hold his breath. Houdini, for instance, who has wonderful breath control, can remain under water for only five minutes.

Of what use are these demonstrations? The reader must judge for himself. The fakir has dramatized for us the soul's struggle for control of our physical nature. Our body has a right to health. Can we win it for ourselves? Are pills, massage and artificial light more than make-shifts? As Dr. Dorsey says in WHY WE BEHAVE LIKE HUMAN BEINGS, evolution depends on our "capacity to modify and delay reactions according to experience." That is exactly what the fakir does.

F. YEATS-BROWN.

OCCIDENTAL HYPNOTISM
(How a Westerner can master the Mind of Man)

(Based upon a lecture and a demonstration of Occidental Hypnotism given at London, Bridlington, Hong Kong and Canton, on various dates under scientific auspices.)

Nearly every great discovery first appears to the average mind as a supernatural manifestation. Indeed, it is supernatural in the best sense of the term, for it is an addition to humanity's knowledge of the Natural.

When Galileo invented the telescope he was accused of magic-mongering by the learned men of his day. In a famous letter to Kepler he told the story of how a learned Doctor at Pisa University turned away in pious horror from his telescope and would not look through such a blasphemous instrument. "How I wish you were here with me to have a good laugh," he wrote.

That is how all pioneers feel about the nervous mass of humanity who cringe before the new knowledge, or who, through their accredited Priesthoods, turn upon the discoverer and castigate him. Oh! for a friend who understands that there is nothing wicked or blasphemous about this new knowledge! Oh! for just one man who could relieve my mind by having a good laugh at the expense of those who laugh so heartily, and with so little reason, at my expense! Is that not the cry of the innovator in all ages?

The power of mind, so long derided by the learned men of the West, is now fast becoming a cardinal point in all the sciences of the world. Hypnotism, the telepathic connection and control of one mind by another, is now being used for the good of the race.

"Dangerous!" say people, when they find they can no longer say, "Ridiculous!" That is their last line of defence, now as always.

Of course, hypnotism is dangerous—in the wrong hands. So is gunpowder, so is arsenic, so is a bread-knife. Even a baby's bottle could be ground up and made into a deadly poison. There is nothing good or bad but thinking makes it so, said Shakespeare, and this applies to hypnotism as to everything else.

The more you know about your own mind and the mind of your neighbour, the more you realize that we are all truly sons of one Great Universal God, and reflections of His Universal Mind. With that knowledge comes peace, and with peace comes the Spirit of God to give us moral power beyond the ability of any knowledge to break—for in the Mind of God knowledge and power are balanced in perfect harmony, and even the suggestion of the possibility of such an unbalance would constitute an intolerable blasphemy against the Holy Spirit.

CHAPTER SEVEN

IN a previous lecture I have described to you the basis and the method of Oriental Hypnotism. If you have understood what I have said in regard to this, you will know that it harnesses up the basic "illusion-stuff" (to coin a phrase) of which the universe is built. This fact the oriental hypnotist fully understands. But the Western man has to progress slowly out of his long sleep of materialism. He cannot face facts so sharply opposed to his whole philosophy of life. He has to begin by treating hypnotism as though it were some incidental psychological manifestation. Everyone comes to knowledge in their own way, and everyone's way to knowledge is very largely conditioned by the age in which they live, and by what the general consent of their age accepts. If the Westerner refuses to acknowledge any wisdom except the wisdom of modern science, well then, he must be approached in another way. Let him keep his belief for the moment that the mind is a "sort of luminosity of the brain" and let him explain hypnotism by saying, for example, that it is a method of controlling that "brain luminosity." What does it matter so long as he accepts hypnotism as a fact? It will not be long before the contradictory nature of his materialistic premises will be revealed by hypnotism. Let the Western man come to wisdom in his own way—it is the only way he can come to it!

On the assumption, then, that Western men need approaching in Western ways, let us tackle the question of hypnotism in a way that needs no highly developed Oriental philosophy to support it. Let us give the man the thing he can believe. But do not for one moment believe that this Occidental method can be compared with the methods of the East. The one is to the other what a one-stringed fiddle is to a Philharmonic Orchestra.

The method I will describe, and also demonstrate, to you is my own.* It has never before been used by any other hypnotist-physician. Let me describe to you the exact details of an hypnotic *séance* as carried through by me either in the mental hospital, or in a consulting-room, or in an institute for psychic research.

The patient enters a quiet, cosy room very dimly lit by a one-candle-power red lamp having a little orange towards the top. An easy-chair or examination couch is suitably arranged with cushions, and so placed that the hypnologist is on the left side of the patient. The patient is instructed to relax, and then for three minutes, soft melodious music is played on a radio-gramophone, using a fibre needle, and with the motor set to 68 revolutions per minute.

The patient is now instructed to take deep breaths, to hold each breath as long as he can, and to picture himself falling asleep. He is told to make a mental picture of himself fast asleep in bed and to fix this picture between his eyes— on the *glabella*. Whilst he is doing this, the other side of the record† is played, being run as before at a speed not greater than *68* revolutions per minute, instead of the 78 recommended by the makers.

---

* At the lecture on which this chapter is based a complete demonstration of hypnotism was given by the Author.

† On the particular record which I use, the tune "Rose Mousse" is on one side and "My Dream" is on the reverse. (Columbia Record).

I now employ the "Cannon hypnoscope,"* and use one of its five coloured lights as an object for the patient to fix his gaze upon. Blue is used for giving etheric vibrations of power to the introverted, self-centred, Schizoid type of person; Orange is used in cases of depression and melancholia; Sunlight in ordinary cases; Emerald Green in cases of excitement and for very "nervy" people; Red (with infra-red) for hypnotizing mediums, or for the production of psychic phenomena. This is a general rule, though under certain circumstances I vary the colour.

The patient fixes his gaze upon the light, which I hold above his eyes, at a distance so that the focus of the light just amply covers both retinæ, and high enough to ensure that the eyes are looking up at it with a certain amount of strain—so that the whites of the eyes below the pupils can be seen.

The suggestions of sleep are now made in *slow*, *monotonous* and *forceful* tones, and in a peacefully rhythmic metre, something like this:

Your a*rms* and-your *legs* are-becoming *warm*-er-and *warmer*—*heav*ier and *heav*ier—and *now*-a-*feel*ing-of *numb*ness-is-creeping *over*-your-arms-and your *legs* and-every *mom*ent you are feeling *more* and more *tired*. Now your *eyes* are-getting-very *tired*, they are be*ginn*ing to *water*—the *eye*-

---

* Made by John Weiss & Son, of 287 Oxford Street, W.1. (I have no financial interest in my invention).

lids are *get*ting very very *heav*y, just like *lead*,
and-are *now* so-very *heavy* that you-can-no-
longer *keep* your-eyes *op*en.*

Should the eyes not close, then I command
the patient in these slow, monotonous, rhythmic
tones of voice, to close the eyes each time I
count, and to let the eyes open again after each
count, when they will still see the light. I
count up to ten, and repeat it even more than
ten times ten if necessary, as it is in some otherwise non-hypnotizable cases. I continue to
count until the eyelids seem to stick, and until
the patient begins to open and close them at the
wrong times. Gradually they only half open, and
then at last they don't open at all, although one
can often observe the patient making a struggling
attempt to open his eyes without success.

The patient is now told to cease to pay any
attention to what I say; and to cease to be able
to hear any other sounds, noises or voices. He
is now told to breathe more deeply, more easily,
and more regularly.

I continue: "Now let your mind wander or
just let it go blank and forget you are here.
Nevertheless your mind will carry out all my
commands. As I stroke this arm " (the one
nearest to me) "from the shoulder to the finger-
tips" (at intervals of one second) "it begins to get
stiffer and stiffer, and you fall still more deeply
to sleep. You are now so fast asleep that you

---

* An attempt has been made to convey the metre by dashes and
italics.

can only hear what *I* say and you can only answer *me*." I now ask him if he can hear me speak, to which he usually replies, "Y-e-es." The witness is then told to ask the subject some interesting question which might put him off his guard, but no reply is made. If, however, I ask the same question he will answer me instantly.

I now say: "You find that not only your left arm" (the one I had been stroking) "but your right arm is also getting stiffer and stiffer and your legs also are getting stiffer and stiffer: in fact your whole body is getting very stiff" (the patient is now in a cataleptic state and can be placed, if so desired, and after testing the extent of the catalepsy, with his neck on one chair and his ankles on another, and one, two or three persons can actually stand on the hypnotized patient without harm or discomfort. The patient's hand can be placed in any direction, and the patient told he cannot move that hand, and that if he tries to move it, it gets still more and more fixed in the position in which it has been placed.) "Now I take hold of your hand and as I raise it in the air, it gets heavier and heavier, and is now so very heavy that when I let go it will fall into your lap heavily, just like a stone." (I now let go of the hand when it falls rapidly and heavily into the lap just as if it did not belong to the patient.) "Now all your limbs and body are quite limp and you now pass into the deep trance or sleep

state and will not be able to remember afterwards anything that I have said or done."

From the very beginning of the experiment
*my right hand has rested firmly on the forehead of the
patient*, and I now spend twenty minutes making
carefully worded suggestions, and all the time
picturing the result of those suggestions on to
the *glabella* of the patient. At the end of this
time, I stroke my left hand across the patient's
waist in front, between the chest and abdomen
(from right to left), suggesting to him at the
same time that there is a feeling of warmth, a
glow; and that as he thinks of this warmth, the
heat spreads all over his body, and as it does so
there is a great feeling of well-being, physical
fitness, mental alertness, of wonderful con-
tentedness, and at the same time an urge to get
on in the world and live a good and noble life
to the honour and glory of God and his own
country and to his family's credit. Then I tell
him that he will not be able to open his eyes
until I have counted up to seven, which I do
in the same, slow, monotonous, rhythmic tones
that I have used throughout the sitting; and
as I say "seven," I once more play the light
of my hypnoscope upon his countenance—
indeed most of my patients have no knowledge that the light has ever been removed
during the sitting. I then let the patient rest
awhile with his eyes open once more and
during these few moments look intently at his
glabella, and strongly and telepathically suggest

on to his mind pictures of all that is good for him, not outlining in detail what he must experience, but mentally opening his consciousness to the great, good, and noble things of life.

The patient rises from that couch a better and more balanced creature, and walks out into a new and greater world feeling a new and greater being.

He has been subjected to a process of "spring-cleaning" so that his "little cup of water," in which the great "Sun" of the Universal Mind reflects its own infinite nature, may not oppose the radiance of that sun by its "filthy" condition. We all need this mental cleaning. It needs to become a cardinal point of our education, our religion, our science and our politics.

We are a doomed race unless *you* follow up the clue which these talks have given to you. For it is upon YOU that the fate of the race depends! The Power is in YOU to be the man to lead the world to Truth! It is in YOU to be a leader of men! It is in YOU to be great! For unless men *do* arise, girt about with the strength of the Great God and determined to so lead men back to Truth, we shall wander on and on in search of happiness and pleasure and power, and gain instead a husk of pain.

The world is looking to the body for pleasure, and to the world in which that body lives. But the world of the body is but a world of echoes—

not realities. It is by living in the mind and the
world of the mind that we find real pleasure.
We cannot do that until we can help other
people to clear their minds of those echoes of
the past, and to lay hold on a greater reality
than they now see.

Hypnosis is, indeed, a God-given faculty
which may be developed by all men. In some
degree we all practise it daily. We all lend our
weight to the common hypnotic beliefs of the
world. We are all to that degree hypnotists.
We daily help to hypnotize ourselves and one
another into the belief that we must dress, and
act, and think in such and such a fashion, and
in another age we should be just as ready to
break that hypnotic spell and supplant it by
another.

Every class, every creed; all nationalism and
sectarianism, is but a collective hypnotism.
And every founder of a class, every creator of
a creed, every man who fosters a nationalistic
spirit or makes a sect, is actually an arch-
hypnotist. Every Empire is a dream—a
dream of power, and glory and adventure
which dominates the minds of the millions who
live under its spell. Change the hypnotic
spell and the dream changes. That is why all
great founders of Empires are called spell-
binders: yea! and so are the great Empire-
breakers; the revolutionaries, for they trade
upon the dissent in the minds of the masses
to make their own dream come true. How

beautifully the poet described this when he said:—

> *We, in the ages lying*
> *In the buried past of the earth,*
> *Built Nineveh with our sighing,*
> *And Babel itself with our mirth;*
> *And o'erthrew them with prophesying*
> *To the old of the new world's worth:*
> *For each age is a dream that is dying*
> *Or one that is coming to birth.*

Our daily task, to which all our efforts and our prayers should be directed, is that we may never be caught in a wrong hypnotic circle, but that we be always left free to pursue the highest and best road.

From a medical point of view, hypnotism is invaluable, and its fringe has only yet been touched. Speaking as a medical man, I will prophesy that in ten years' time a complete revolution will have taken place in medicine in regard to hypnotism and mediumship.

Medical knowledge is very necessary for the practice of the art, lest some abdominal catastrophe or the like be camouflaged by its power, and the sufferer be relieved of his pain but not of the essential defect. Skilled hands are necessary for the curative practice of hypnosis, and in all cases it demands the highest integrity and moral rectitude. In such hands it is the greatest power for good upon earth.

A final word about the name itself. HYP-
NOTISM is not a good word for the manifestation
which we have been discussing. It comes from
the Greek word *hypnos*, meaning sleep, but the
state of mind of the hypnotized person is so
different from that of a sleeping person that
there is real need for a sharp differentiation
between the two.

A state of mind in which telepathy, clair-
voyance, clairaudience, and other occult faculties manifest themselves, is indeed worthy of
another name. I would suggest, therefore, that
we replace the word "hypnotism" by the term
—THE PSYCHIC STATE.

THE SCIENCE OF THE KINGDOM

A Study of the Mind, the Universe, Reincarnation,
the Prophecies of the Bible, the meaning of Numbers
and of the Book of Revelation.

(Based upon a lecture given at Bridlington on the 30th July, 1934.)

*Is reincarnation a fact? Do we live again? Is there a
grand cycle of Life which knows of no mortality? These
questions are being asked with a greater insistence every day,
and an ever-growing volume of discussion rages around
them and around similar questions.*

*There are two kinds of discussion upon these subjects.
One consists of mere argument which depends for its success
upon our prowess in dialectic methods. The other is
scientific, but whilst being based upon the methods of
science, it is not based upon a materialistic theory.*

*This lecture is based upon research. Research! The
mind of the reader at once flies to the challenge. What sort
of research? By what means do you replace the laboratory
of the physicist and the chemist? What takes the place of
the microscope and the telescope, the test tube and the
oscillagraph?*

*The scientific, or pseudo-scientific, literature of recent
years has made much of inventions yet to come which would
startle the world with their overcoming of Time and Space.
The scenes and voices of the Past would be brought to life
in the Present. The super-radio of the novelist of " Time-
to-Come" and the Time Machine of H. G. Wells, spring to
the mind as one reads such forecasts.*

*But when it is realized that even our present-day inventions
are but outward symbols of powers latent in our own minds
and bodies, then our point of view instantly changes. When*

we see that the telephone is but a shadow of our own nervous system; that the radio is an externalization of our undeveloped telepathic powers; that every pump, piston, and valve in the mechanical world was foreshadowed long ages ago in the human mind-body; then we begin to see that there is no need for us to look outside our own bodies for the great new inventions of the future—nor, indeed, for the instruments wherewith the future laboratory will be fitted. The nature of Life and its processes lies for ever outside the ken of the physicist and his instruments: it is to the psychic researcher that the secrets of Life yield up their treasure.

Jesus said, The Kingdom of Heaven is within you. Yes, and the apparatus necessary for the study of that Kingdom is within you, too; for the Kingdom is complete.

This lecture is based upon research carried out by utilizing the powers of the human mind. It is not claimed that this is the first time such research has been made, for the science of the Kingdom, as truly as the science of its Earth-shadow, is built up by the steady work of many, both visible and invisible, who are working in the love of Truth.

By observing the marvellous action and reaction of the human mind when its sensitivity is heightened by being placed in the psychic state, there has been gathered together an amazing body of evidence concerning things too often treated by the Western mind as being matters of speculation or even of hysteria.

This new laboratory of the future! It is the laboratory of the scientist of the Kingdom of Heaven: the scientist who will enable knowledge to be added to faith and hope—thus bringing divine Wisdom to mankind.

THE GREAT CHAPTER

LESSONS FROM THE UNIVERSAL MIND

THE day is far spent and night is beginning to lower. Darkness creeps over the land and the night cometh; not to stay—but for a while. For to-morrow the sun once more shall rise and another day will be upon us, to be followed by another night and yet another day. This is a parable of the endless life of man. Listen to the story, the true story, of the life-everlasting, in which there is no death, but an Eternity.

When we die, are we extinct? What happens after death? These are great questions, and to-day they are engaging the attention of men as never before in the history of the world.

When we ask the trance subject if immortality is a fact, does there not come back to us an answering voice:

We do not die! We live on through the ages into eternity.

Who are you? we ask the Voice; and it replies, *I am a Voice.*

But, we say, *that conveys nothing to our mind. What, after all, is the value of a voice with no personality behind it?*

In reply we hear these searching words:

You do not seem to understand.   The voice is the

instrument whereby we, The Greater World, can make known unto you the great Truths of Eternity in language form. Do you not remember that when John the·Baptist was in trance he said, in answer to the question, 'Who are you?' 'I am a Voice crying out in the wilderness'?—in the wilderness of humanity's ignorance and wilful rejection.

Ah! Now we begin to understand. This is only a Voice, but it has the power of Eternity behind it. Yet we are constrained to ask again, *What then is Eternity?*

Immediately the answer comes:

Eternity means freedom from Time and Space. Eternity means the cessation of limitation—when you have no physical body, and when "material" objects no longer exist for you. Indeed, matter is the only condition of life that needs Time and Space, because its very foundation consists of the relationship existing between these two factors, as the Einstein theory demonstrates so effectively.

Then the real Self, the mind and personality of man, exists apart from this world of Time and Space? we ask.

Assuredly it does, the Voice answers. *But it exists in a form of manifestation which the human body has no physical senses to perceive. Likewise, it expresses its thoughts by vibrations of colour and of music in the Ether, and does not rely upon the crude methods of clattering the tongue against the roof of the mouth, and the teeth, and in sharp regulated gusts of air.*

The Ether in which all unseen Life exists is not a material thing; it is an invisible fluid which "material" electricity as nearly as possible foreshadows. It is the basis of all that exists. Remove the Ether from your body and that body crumbles into dust. Remove the Ether from the dust, and the dust has no longer an existence as dust. You cannot see the Ether any more than you can see the wind that shakes the trees: all you can sense by means of your body are the forms and the forces which are built up by Etheric vibrations. When these vibrations change or appear to cease, the form disappears, yet the Ether continues to exist, just as the ocean continues to exist when the waves can no longer be seen, and seem to have disappeared. Compare the Ether with an ocean, and compare "matter" with waves upon its surface, and you have a very good symbol upon which to exercise your mind.

Then the mind is not the brain of man? we ask.

The Voice answers: *No, the brain is the manifestation of Ether in a certain condition of sensitivity to its own forms and vibrations. In this sensitive state it forms a kind of wireless set whereby Etheric vibrations are picked up and transformed into nerve-currents which, in turn, can cause the production of "material" phenomena, such as sound waves or bodily action. So, you see, the brain is not really different from the vibrations it records. It is all a question of degree. All Life is one and indivisible, and so-called matter and its real substance are not divided in the sight of the Eternal God, for the difference between them lies not in any reality but in their appearance to us. This is why the Philosophers have always said that "life is a dream." It is, but we must make it a real dream, and a beautiful one.* In this way does the Voice from the Greater World speak to us its message of unity and eternal life.

The unity of Life is the doctrine upon which all my advice to you is based. See how it explains the practical advice I have given you in regard to the control of your thought. Let us illustrate this by means of a simple experiment.

Let us take a glass jug half filled with water, and immerse in it, to three-quarters of its area, a large handkerchief. Here we have a good symbol of the human mind—the fabric below the water representing the unconscious mind of man, and the dry quarter representing his conscious mind. Let us now place a piece of lump sugar upon the dry part of the hand-kerchief. This represents a thought held in the conscious mind. Observe what happens! It causes only a little impression on the hand-kerchief. The sweetness of the sugar is not absorbed by the handkerchief. This is pre-cisely what happens when a thought is, for a fleeting moment, held by our conscious minds. It does not usually affect us to any great extent and if we can cast that thought out of our minds it goes without having accomplished very much for us, good or bad.

Now let us depress the handkerchief until the whole of it is below the surface of the water, carrying with it the lump of sugar. Observe now what happens! The sugar rapidly dis-solves into the water and, in this state, it now sweetens the water and the whole of the hand-

kerchief as well. This is a very good analogy of
what happens when a person falls asleep with
a thought held clearly in the conscious mind:
the thought is borne down into the unconscious
mind where it pervades, in a most effective
manner, the whole mind of the sleeper. Remember this when you are trying to impress upon
your mind the great future you desire to achieve.

Just as the water in the jug is related to all the
water in the world so is your mind related to
Mind and if you understand this fact you will be
able to understand the relation between your
own total mind (conscious and subconscious) and
the Eternal and Universal Mind of God. Once
you see how true this analogy is, you will never be
able to say again that a man can die.   Indeed,
there is not, and cannot be, any room in the
Universe for such an idea as death.

Consider the rose! Think how it blooms;
refreshing and beautifying the world with its
colour and perfume! When the autumn comes
and the bloom and the perfume disappear, we
say that the rose is "dead"; but is this a correct
statement of the facts? Indeed it is not! For
the tree remains, and out of the depths of winter
it emerges with its precious burden held safely for
the glory of another summer, and once again the
bloom charms our eyes, and once again the perfume pervades the atmosphere with its fragrance.

But suppose the rose-tree itself died! What
then? Where then would be the colour and
the perfume? Deprived of their parent stem,

what would be their fate? We know that from remnants left behind in the earth a new tree would sometime spring forth, and give the lie to the belief that death had conquered the rose.

Yet again, supposing every rose-tree in the world were consumed by fire! Would that not be the end of the rose? How could it be? Do we not know that the great complex Idea of which this world is formed is beyond the reach of fire: in this great unseen Etheric world exists the perfect source of every form of Life, and of every idea ever manifested upon earth. In this Etheric world death has no meaning.

Are we to suppose that what applies to the rose does not apply with equal force to us? If we were less than a rose, might we not even then hope to bloom again in a new summer? But, since we are more than the rose, can we not then be sure that there is an ever warmer summer for us in which to bloom, and a more glorious life in store for us in days that are to come!

Yes, we may be sure of it. It is made plain on every hand to those who have eyes to see and ears to hear. Even this little story of the rose provides us with a perfect assurance of the deathless nature of man. It also illustrates very vividly the threefold nature of man: the Physical, the Astral, and the Etheric. The rose itself illustrates the nature of the physical body; the tree is the symbol of the astral body which can raise up another physical body (rose) should it be destroyed; and the unseen reality of the

Eternal Rose Idea represents the Etheric body, which is the perfect shape and pattern of Man. It is interesting to note that the Astral body will often show signs of disease for a time after being separated from its physical shadow, but the Etheric body is never anything but perfect; it is Divine!

The foregoing picture of man's threefold nature is in perfect accordance with the symbolism given to you in an earlier chapter on ORIENTAL HYPNOTISM. Therein the visible universe was likened to the reflection of a universal Sun in numerous little cups of water. In the present chapter the Etheric reality takes the place of the Sun; the Astral body is the reflection; and man's physical body is used instead of the symbol of the cups of water. Different aspects of the one underlying reality require different symbols to express them, and the reader should endeavour to work out for himself the coherency which exists between the different symbols which have been painted and presented in the different chapters.

There is no death! That is the supreme message which this chapter has for you! What a profound change would come over the whole world if that lesson were well and truly learned! Suicide and murder would cease. Men would be afraid to put the claims of warfare before the claims of their immortal souls. For everyone would know as a matter of common knowledge that to hurl men into unconsciousness with all their faults upon them is a dreadful business, fraught with future terror for the world.

What a lesson the would-be suicide can learn from the fact that we do not, cannot, die! He would then know that suicide, so far from ending his miseries, would plunge him into a dilemma ten thousand times worse than the one from which he seeks to escape—a dilemma from which escape would be ten thousand times harder than before.

The murderer, too, pays for his crime a million times more fully than any capital punishment could ever hope to make him do. In fact, so far from punishing the murderer, society is really punishing itself when it resorts to capital punishment, since the loss of the physical body, by hanging or by any other method, merely plunges the murderer's mind into the Unconscious where his murderous ideas, like the lump of sugar in our previous analogy, are able to spread into the mental atmosphere of the world. In this way the "dead" murderer can take possession of other people's bodies during the sleep state, or during periods of dissociation,* and can thus cause more murders and suicides.

---

* Dissociation is a word used to describe a condition wherein the conscious and the unconscious minds are not in association the one with the other. In this state there is always a danger of possession by another vagrant or unclean "spirit." The phenomenon of possession is a well-attested fact of psychic science, as well as being a widely held religious belief. Hence one more link between the Old Science and the New.

I would, therefore, appeal with all my heart to the Powers That Be to abolish capital punishment, and to replace it with reformed methods (not of punishment, for that is based upon an archaic morality) such as, for example, psychic treatment, whereby the sinner could be purged of his malady.

MEMORY AND PAST LIVES

Now it is time that you should know of some of the experiments which I have conducted in co-operation with a scientific research committee composed for the most part of well-known medical and scientific men, and also of leading figures in society. The committee now includes such well-known people as Dr. E. T. Jensen, and Dr. Radwan, who is well known in Vienna, the U.S.A., Russia and Germany.

Our research work is conducted by the use of hypnotic subjects whom we put into an hypnotic trance, and by whose hyper-sensitive minds we can tap the records of the past, and even peep into the future—proving thereby among other things that Time and Space have no real existence and are only relative.

Let me give you a brief record of one of our recent sittings. A middle-aged woman, whom none of the committee knew, was put into a deep trance. When in this psychic state we tested her memory of the past by suggesting to her that she was living at a certain time in the past. We started her on August 4th, 1924, which was ten years previous to the date of our sitting, and found that she was able to re-enact her experiences of ten years ago—not as though she were witnessing a film of the past, nor, indeed, as though she were performing a feat of memory, but as though she were actually living in the past of ten years ago. After we had satisfied ourselves with the record thus obtained, we pushed her back another ten years, to the 4th of August, 1914. Once again she went through the experiences of that time, and she vividly recalled the shadow that was overhanging Britain on that afternoon of our entry into the last Great War.

After this, we suggested her back further and further into the past by ten-year steps at a time, and finally, by single years, right back to the day of her birth. First of all she described her first bath after birth, and this she did by saying that she was "in the water" and that she could not breathe because the "umbilical cord" had been strangling her. After this we pushed her still further back into Time until we arrived at a moment which was half an hour prior to her actual birth. At this point she cried out that all was dark, and she described sounds which may well have been the noise of blood rushing through the arteries. As she was born she shouted, "I'm out!"

She was able to relate where her mother was, and when asked if she could see her mother

she replied, "No!" But she added that she
knew where her mother was because there was
a ray of light connecting herself with her
mother, but not with anyone else in the room.
The subject then described herself as being in
a cradle by the fire. She said there was a nurse
in the room, a fact which she knew by the way
in which that person was attending to her
mother. Our Medium described the bedroom
in which she was born, although she was, as
it were, only "half an hour old." The subject
was also able to tell us the name of the house
in which she was born, and the name of the
street in which the house stood, though to do this
she had to "go out of the house" and "look"
at the names of both the street and the house.

Before I describe the further results of this
experiment, I would point out an extraordinary
fact of great interest. The Subject, although
she is actually living and enacting the Past,
even to the extent of curling up into a pre-
natal attitude, speaks in a normal but childlike voice. Moreover, when in the psychic
state, this and other subjects will use terms and
phrases which are either totally unknown to
them in the waking state, or at least, are by no
means habitually employed by them. In the
case of the woman now under review, I am
quite sure that she did not in her ordinary
conversation employ such terms as "umbilical
cord," for example. In describing her birth she
spoke in a baby's tone and manner.

Another finding of great importance has been our observation of the behaviour of a subject who was an unwanted child. In such cases the subject does not see a ray of light connecting her with her mother, but sees instead a black cloud where the mother is, and it cries and cries, knowing that it is not wanted. In such cases the subjects always complain that the Earth-world is cold and dark. Think of this terrible happening! Is it possible that any married couple would ever bring an unwanted child into the world if they knew that their thoughts were being read, not only by the newborn babe, but by the unborn child as well? Knowing this great truth, would not every mother and father think only kind thoughts, and loving thoughts about their "happy event" (which, indeed, it should be) and also about one another. What a difference this would make to the world! Can you imagine what a marvellous new world would arise from a generation of children born in complete love and harmony? Even in this way the planet Earth could be changed. Let all preachers and teachers proclaim this homely yet vital information to the whole world, for there is no surer way of teaching the supreme lesson that God is Love and that all loving thoughts are of Him.

By suggesting to our subject that she was existing still further and further back in Time we obtained from her full details of her gestation and of the building up of her body. The date of her conception was also given to us in a like manner.

Then we pushed her back to a time beyond the conception of her present body, and in reply to the question, "Where are you now?" the answer came, "I am away up in the sky." I retorted by saying that this meant nothing to me, and "What I want to know is, exactly where are you?" The reply then came that she was in *The Garden of Waiting*, and there followed a description of how all. etheric or spirit forms who were ready to reincarnate spent two years in this place awaiting their rebirth into another physical body. She told us of the beauty of this *Garden of Waiting*, and described the colours as being more beautiful than anything she had ever seen on earth. When asked what she did in this place, she replied, "We are guarded and protected by 'The White Brothers' and 'The Blue Sisters' (sic) whose task it is to see that the spirit enters into the physical body intended for it." It was explained that when one entered into a female body the *Blue Sisters* stood around, and the *White Brothers* stood afar off: the reverse being the procedure whan a male body was being entered.

The subject was then asked if there was any choice in the matter of the body into which an entity was being reincarnated. She replied that there was no choice, but that it all depended upon how one had lived in one's past life on earth and in the intermediary life on the other planets as to what body and what station of life one would inhabit in the next incarnation.

The following letter which appeared in the August 10th issue of LIGHT makes interesting and confirmatory reading.

Sir,

Having read in your issue of July 27th Dr. Alexander Cannon's letter, in which he states that, according to his information, people of the present day have lived before during the Roman period and were usually murdered, I think that the following facts may be of interest.

In the year 1931, through an entranced medium, I was given a detailed account of my last earth life. It was that of a Roman woman, in the second century A.D., and was ended by her murder, or execution, for having broken a certain law. This life was spontaneously described to me again, in July 1932, by another trance Medium, who has never met the first. I was also told that souls before being reborn, "wait in a place of preparation for earth return." This corresponds with Dr. Cannon's "Garden of Waiting," and seems to be a striking coincidence if nothing more.

I have the dated records of my sittings, taken down by me at the time. Neither of the Mediums or myself were believers in reincarnation, though quite unbiased. I was told that some "accidental souls" do not reincarnate, but live, on leaving the earth, for longer or shorter periods in a part of the astral plane which is a reflection or dream copy of the physical world; after which they become merged in their groups, losing to a

*great extent their individuality. This might account
for differences of opinion among communicators.*

E. K.

We then took the subject's memory back
another five years and found that she was then
living on the planet Venus.

THE PLANET VENUS

Here, however, a question arose which caused
us some little difficulty at first. The subject
pointed out that our computations were based
upon Earth-time and that this created a confusion because there was no time-factor on
Venus in the sense known on Earth.

Some interesting details were given as to the
nature of life on Venus. I asked her what went
on there, and she replied that instruction in the
art of living was the main activity, also she
indicated that work as we know it on Earth did
not exist on that planet. She told us that the
light on Venus was constant and extremely
brilliant; so brilliant, in fact, that our Earth
was described as being, even on the brightest
day, black or dark in comparison with it.
She continued to relate facts about Venus, and
said that the "vegetation" on the planet dif-
fered greatly from that of the earth. She
described the trees, for example, as being
"metallic" in appearance. I interrupted, and
remarked that it was absurd to speak of trees
being made of metal, and I scornfully implied

that there was no sense in it. She retorted that there was indeed plenty of sense in it, and pointed out that there were "metallic trees" on the Earth and reminded me of the "lead tree" which many a schoolboy has built.

Anyone who doubts this should try the following experiment for themselves: get a wide-necked bottle, and pour into it a clear acidulated solution of lead acetate. Fix a piece of copper wire to the cork, and on the other end of the wire attach a strip of zinc—in such a position that when the cork is fitted, the zinc will be in the centre of the lead acetate. As soon as the cork is in position the copper wire will commence to be covered with a deposit of zinc which resembles a fine moss, and which, after a time, grows into a likeness of a tree, having main branches, smaller branches, and foliage.

This simple experiment, well known to chemists, was quite unknown to the Medium, though she instructed me in a most imperious tone to try it when I criticized her comment about there being "metallic trees" on Venus. The chemical and mineral worlds of the Earth furnish us with many instances of the growth and development of forms closely resembling those assumed by the vegetable world. What is known as "metallic vegetation," as depicted by "the lead tree" for example, gives us an interesting side-light upon the uniformity of Nature. It is a mistake to suppose that minerals and chemicals have no life. Everything in the Universe is alive if only we knew it, so most assuredly everything in this little Earth is alive. Crystals are born: They grow and may be killed by chemicals or by electric shock. Even rudimentary sex is shown to exist among crystals: in fact, crystallization is really a birth, the crystal being formed in the "mother" liquor, wherein it is regularly and systematically built up according to a clearly defined plan. Furthermore, the germ from which a crystal grows can be rendered incapable of growth by a process of sterilization. Once this fact is understood, the whole world takes on a new and entrancing aspect, especially when it is realized that our hardest rocks and metals are composed of crystals, and that the soil of the Earth is but the crumbled remains of rocks.

There is no point at which we can draw a line between the living and the non-living. Every form of life shades off imperceptibly into the next. Plants prey upon others; chemicals can be poisoned or injured; metals get tired, so that razor blades need to be given a rest, motor-engines will "give up" under too prolonged stresses, and tuning-forks lose their vibratory power and period after prolonged use. Machines and tools are living things: have you not heard an expert say that a tool must be properly handled to give of its best? Window glass is subject to disease, especially stained glass, and the disease will spread from pane to pane by a process of infection. Metals also can become diseased by infection, and, in fact, the list of such correspondences in Nature is never ending. Professor Sir Jagada Bose of Calcutta University has proved all things to be alive, and has shown that the same reaction to a given stimulus will within limits be obtained from all forms of so-called matter. Anyone who doubts this great fact should read his amazing book, RESPONSE IN THE LIVING AND NON-LIVING. In short, there seems to be a universal plan or design behind all life which is manifested even by the frost crystals when they build upon our window panes their well-known pictures of leaves and flowers: or by carrots which grow into human shape, or by the humble pansy with a face like a cat. Pause for a moment and think of these things!

THE IMMENSE SOLARIUM

Another thing which the Medium said when questioned on the growth of metallic trees was that the growth and pattern of the tree was controlled by the movement of the planet upon which it was growing. This statement by the Medium might have been passed over by us as too vague for any special notice were it not for the fact that an interesting letter has come to me which I hope to be able to publish in my

next book.* This letter comes from an English-
man who tells the story of how he once visited
a Russian mystic who was a superscientist and
pursued his investigations into Nature without
being handicapped by the tenets of orthodox
materialistic science.   My correspondent des-
cribes how he found at the home of this
mystic Russian "an immense solarium" built
of metal, in which all the planets were represented by iron spheres suitably magnetized to
give each one a pull upon the other roughly
corresponding to the gravitational pull of the
planets. The ball which represented our Earth
was covered with a fine iron dust, and the
solarium was set in motion. To my correspondent's amazement, *as soon as the solarium got into
full motion the iron dust on the "Earth" began to
shape itself into the forms of rudimentary trees and
even of animals.* This letter, coming from a man
of distinction, certainly lends weight to the statement of the Medium under trance.

A PAST LIFE

To return to our experiment! We continued
suggesting to our subject that she was living
further and further back in the deeps of Time,
and each time we took her back in ten-year
steps—of Earth time. The next Earth-life was
recorded in B.C. 98 when the entity had a male
body and was a slave on a Roman galley.

---

* KARMA (The Francis Mott Company).

(Between this Earth life and the present one, incidentally, the entity did not seem to have left Venus.)

Naturally, since we approach each incarnation from its end instead of its beginning, we get the death scenes before the life scenes, and in the case of the B.C. 98 galley-slave existence the death was most dramatic. The subject suddenly began to go blue in the face and to express great agony of mind and body. She writhed in her chair, and her contortions were utterly amazing. The explanation of this, given to us by another witness-subject, was that the galley-slave had been thrown into the water *in chains*, and had been eaten alive by crocodiles. All these scenes were re-enacted in the most astoundingly realistic manner; so much so, indeed, that one could at first scarcely restrain a desire to rush to the aid of the suffering subject, though one knew that her agony was not in "Time-Present" but in "Time-Past." The subject was awakened later none the worse for her experiences, for she had merely been back in the *Mayâ* of Time, which is the Eternal Now, if only we had eyes to see and ears to hear as has the Medium. What greater or more perfect illustration could one have of the illusion of Time?

Still further back in this "B.C. 98 life," we found the galley-slave enchained in a prison cell, and the subject described to us in detail the prison walls and the chains.

During this particular past life I did not pursue the practice of taking the subject back in ten-year steps, but moved her memory-periods back in shorter intervals of time. The result was extremely interesting. Not only were the subject's statements for the most part confirmatory of known Roman history, but there were statements made by her which perfectly filled in some gaps in our knowledge, whilst other statements were contrary to our accepted ideas. For instance, the subject insisted that there were no Roman baths prior to the year B.C. 80, and said that the people did not wash in the ordinary way but annointed themselves daily with oil, the ceremony taking place in public places reserved at noon for the women and at sundown for the men.

Space precludes the inclusion of further details of this particular experiment, for we have many other things to discuss before this last chapter is brought to a close. A general survey of the results of our 140 sittings shows a most interesting constancy. The use of the hyper-sensitive human mind when in a psychic state reveals the existence of knowledge beyond ordinary human ken, and is most emphatically justifying its use in the new Science of Mind.

EXPERIMENTS ARE NOT PROOF

There is a good deal of conflicting evidence in the world on the matters of which I speak.

But this has always been the case when research is in its early stages. I would by no means attempt to be rigidly dogmatic or to place final conclusions upon the experiments so far carried out, but they should in my opinion be made known because they are of such arresting importance. There are many people dabbling in psychic research at the moment who have not the requisite knowledge to enable them to steer clear of the pitfalls. Hence they get into touch with entities that have nothing valid to impart, or they find themselves catching their own reflected thoughts. A man's ability to go under control is no proof of his ability to "control his control" and for years I have insisted upon the danger of auto-hypnosis and have pointed out that no Medium ought to allow himself, or herself, to practise it. Every Medium ought to be hetero-hypnotized, and even then care should be taken to see that the hypnologist is a very competent person. A Medium, like a wireless set (and the analogy is very close), needs to be controlled and "tuned" to the station it is desired to receive.

Examples of the prevailing differences of opinion are given by the two following letters reproduced in part from the columns of LIGHT.

In the issue of July 13th, 1934, Mr. M. Crompton-Smith of Wellington, New Zealand, wrote concerning reincarnation :

In view of the puzzle that it is so often denied in English Circles and affirmed in Continental ones, I asked for an authoritative statement at my own Circle for a second time. On the first occasion, the controls had said that, while they had never known of a case of Reincarnation and did not believe it occurred, they could not pose as authorities, but would try to ascertain for us.

On the second occasion of asking as to Reincarnation, again a high spirit came and answered of his actual knowledge of the subject, and I give question and answer from my practically verbatim notes made at the time (January 15th, 1934).

This is the communication, question and answer:

Question.—*There is the subject of Reincarnation on which communications from your side seem to differ, English Circles chiefly learning that it never occurs, while Continental circles hear that it does. Could we now hear anything authoritative about it? You promised something of the sort on a previous occasion.*

Answer.—*My friend, you were asking if your souls come again upon earth into an earthly body, after they have once left it for the Beyond. I wish to say this—that under no circumstances whatever does the soul come again to Earth. Some think that at times some do; others that it is the regular procedure. But you must know—you who have studied this subject (of communication) as much as you have—that when we pass over at first our knowledge is not much greater than when we left the earth, and if such an one comes to a circle he will give his own thoughts back, as on Earth, not having learned sufficient to realize what he is doing. I do think that probably when people appear to get messages that Reincarnation is a fact, it is because they have made contact with those whose idea it was when on Earth.*

But I have knowledge, and, do not doubt my word—your life, when once lived on earth, is all that is required of you by the Father, and all the rest of it is carried out in the Spheres and not on Earth. I who speak know *what I say, and before I leave you again I wish to say: seek always for truth and fear not to speak the truth when opportunity comes. Seek truth perseveringly, patiently, in all things and your reward will be great, here and on Earth. Farewell my friends, my blessing rest on you and on your seeking.*

To this letter I replied in the issue of July 27th as follows:

THE GARDEN OF WAITING

Sir,
    I have for some time conducted scientific experiments on Reincarnation and must therefore openly state that the information stated by Mr. Crompton-Smith of Wellington, New Zealand, is misleading although obviously written in good faith.

For some time I have used hypnosis in the deep trance state *to ascertain the possibility of proving prophetic dreams, never having believed in such a thing as reincarnation. Nevertheless by my unbiased investigations, I was shown to be wrong. I would like to recall two sittings which took place during the last fortnight in which the following people were present:*

Dr. E. T. Jensen, Dr. Radwan as well as several well-known accredited members of the nobility, and the Mediums used were Miss Canon and Mrs. King. I had not met with the Mediums before, and they were placed in hypnotic trance without previous conversation on any matter whatsoever. The witnesses will testify to evidence pointing to the fact that we (1) *live more than one life;* (2) *live on more than one planet;* (3) *memory persists in the minutest detail from the present day, traced backwards through all our earthly life even to the date of birth, and before that during gestation to conception, and before that to a period of stay (which seems to be constant at two years) in " The Garden of Waiting " protected by the " Blue Sisters " and the " White Brothers," who select our next physical body in accordance with what we deserve from our progression or regression in the past. Previous to having entered " The Garden of Waiting," all my cases have lived for not less than* 300 *and not more than* 2,000 *years on another planet, and the favourite planet is Venus. Going still further back, we come to the time when they were last on Earth, most being here during the Roman period, and they describe their lives most accurately on earth during this period B.C.*

All my subjects to date (although not specially picked except for their suitability to be placed quickly in a deep trance state) state that they were either murdered, or committed suicide during the last earthly life. As I am only on the edge of this research into this fascinating study, it would be premature to draw any conclusion on this point or put forth any theories based on this information.

I wish to insist upon the need for avoiding extremes. Those who give up the search because the evidence conflicts are not worthy of the name of Superscientists, for this is the true title of those who are devoting themselves to the unravelling of these great Truths, and this is true also of those who fly to one extreme or the other. Often that which appears to be a stumbling-block is actually the clue to the Truth. With this great fact clearly before us let us accept the evidence at its true value and press on. We are all of us philosophers in embryo, and here is actual experimental evidence for the mind to work upon. So far as the proof goes, it appears that we have lived upon this Earth before, and that, *ad interim* between our Earth-lives, we have also inhabited other planets. Every subject so far tested mentions Mercury and Venus as the chief of the inhabitable spheres in our system, but they all with one accord deny that they, or anyone else, have ever lived on Mars. They give no reason for this, but also point out that Mars is astronomically the one reddish-coloured planet —which is rather suggestive.

Confirmation of reincarnation will interest those who claim to have a distinct memory of a past life; and it will also interest those who have received at some time in their life the impression that they have seen a certain view before, whereas their personal history makes it clear that they have never been within miles of the scene. The familiarity of these scenes strongly suggests the existence of a subliminal conscious memory of a previous existence. In this connection dreams are a fascinating study.

All the subjects so far used have stated that the Earth is populated not only with physical beings but with astral and etheric beings as well. These are the beings whom I believe are called elementals* and spirits by the Spiritualists.

The existence of other levels of consciousness, and of worlds within worlds which are interpenetrating but not in mutual conscious contact, has not only been stated by the subjects as a matter of fact, but has also been demonstrated by them in ways which permit of no doubt in the matter.

PSYCHOMETRY AND ASTRAL PROJECTION

Let me refer you to one particular subject, a lady, who was not addressed by us in any way until she had given the sitting and who did not remember any of the following incidents after she came out of the trance in which she performed them. Within a few moments of her arrival at our meeting she was put into a deep hypnotic trance and her knowledge was then tested in regard to the personalities constituting our scientific circle. Although the subject did

---

* Elementals are spirits which have never lived on earth in human physical bodies.

not know a single member of that committee, she stated accurately the names, titles, and degrees of every member of the "circle," and gave exact replies to questions concerning the intimate details of their lives.

A photograph was then placed in her hands— a photograph of a person who was then three hundred miles away from us. Although she never opened her eyes to look at the photograph, she told us within a minute who the person was, and gave his name, sex, and his place of residence quite correctly. She also described the room in which he was sitting at that very moment, and also related his movements. Intimate details of his life were also given to us, and in addition certain forecasts of his future. The former were subsequently confirmed, and the minor prophecies concerning his future are, by subsequent events, shown to have been remarkably accurate.

This subject was also used by us to test the power of thought-projection over a distance, and the results of the experiment were highly interesting. We handed her the same photograph that was used in the previous experiment, and she was then commanded to reinforce my thought to this person (then three hundred miles away), whilst I fixed my gaze and my thought intently upon the photograph. The thought which I commanded the subject to project was that of my physical body, and particularly of my eyes, the idea being to try to project a shadow-form of myself across the intervening three hundred miles. Remember that Space does not exist in the astral world.

The result of our experiment was made known to us in an equally interesting manner. We did not have to await reports from a distance: all we had to do was to put yet a second subject into a trance and tell him* to report on the result of our thought-projection on the man three hundred miles away.

At once the second subject calmly stated what was taking place in that geographically far-distant room. *He is glancing round,* was the report. *He seems to feel a draught, and yet he cannot understand it because there is no possible source of a physical draught.*

The wind which this man felt was a psychic wind, and in a few seconds the subject who was reporting to us told us that the man had jumped from his chair and was staring ahead of him in a nervous and half-dazed manner, having seen me vaguely, but my eyes very clearly. A few seconds later still the subject said, *He has turned tail and is running out of the room.*

Then a most interesting thing happened: the first subject immediately jumped out of her chair and tried to run after the man who was three hundred miles away, thus showing the reaction of the astral body upon the physical body even when "at a great distance."

---

* Male subjects are also used.

The second subject who had acted as our hypnotic witness of the distant event, then described how the man had seen my eyes and then my face, and had rushed from the room in terror and had refused to return to it again that evening. Later, an independent witness confirmed these facts.

The reader will see that my remarks in this chapter are not based upon supposition, but upon tested evidence which has been most remarkably and encouragingly constant throughout the sittings so far carried through. One hundred and thirty of the sittings have shown identical findings, and such evidence as this defies the attacks of the most materialistic doctrinaires and cannot lightly be passed over by even the most hardened cynic. It has been shown in these sittings that the average person may live seven times on Earth as a man and seven times as a woman, thus completing a full cycle of seven positives (males) and seven negatives (females) which, taken in conjunction one with the other, makes up a complete cycle of seven waves. There is an average interval of one thousand Earth-years between each Earth-life, during which intervals the entity achieves astral life on other planets where it inhabits new "planetary bodies."

THE END OF THE WORLD

The subjects have told us almost unanimously that the "end of the world" is near at hand. They say that there has been at least one such catastrophe before, and the world was then consumed in a gigantic conflagration. They also say that the mysterious "first man" called Adam in the Jewish Chronicles, and referred to in almost all ancient records of Creation, was a reference to the first being to repopulate the world after the conflagration.

To this statement I have always posed the same question: How can you repopulate the world after complete destruction? and to this question the reply has always been that the Creator can create when and where He will. It has also been pointed out that small germs and other forms of life are "created" out of "nothing" in unclean places, and further questioning on the subject has drawn forth the following comment as regards materialization.

MATERIALIZATIONS

They draw attention to the phenomenon of materialization which has been popularized by psychics and spiritualists, and say that if human beings can do these things, then greater things are possible to God. When asked to explain the nature of materializations, the subjects state that it is due to a thought being

held intently and long enough in the mind.*
It was emphasized by the subjects that this
phenomenon was a human representation of
the process whereby the Almighty creates
His Universe—note that I say "creates" and
not "created." This argument is not one
to be lightly dismissed, and I have set it down
as one of the more easily understood and
fundamental statements made by the subjects.

SCIENCE OF THE KINGDOM OF GOD

This brief review of our actual experimental
work must suffice, at least, for this book. There
is so much to be written; so many things to be
achieved; so many things that "come through"
which could not be set down in cold print for
public consumption, as yet. I say this because
there are things known to me which, properly
interpreted, lift up the mind and reveal the
Kingdom of Heaven in its true sense, but
which would, if fanatically interpreted, bring
ruin and devastation of mind where only good
inheres. These great psychic matters touch the
heights and the depths of the soul: they are
not mere matters of science as we understand
the term, for they suggest the existence of a
new Science—the Science of the Kingdom of
God.

It is not yet realized that psychology, as
interpreted by the Western psychologists, is

---

* See reference to *Mayā* in chapters one and six.

indeed but a matter of surface-scratching—great as even that achievement may be in its own time and place. Western psychology deals with the conscious and sub-conscious human mind: poor little fleeting ripple of consciousness upon those vast unknown oceans of the Universal Soul-Mind! How can we limit ourselves to such a science? Indeed, it is impossible to do so unless we ignore the great ocean and only look at the waves. This is, in fact, just what has been done. The great ocean of the Universal Mind has been pushed aside and dismissed by Western psychology simply by calling it grand names.

Experiments such as ours push the enquiry deeper than does mere Western psychology. We scratch harder than that, and in piercing beneath the veneer of the human consciousness we find ourselves tapping a universal force. This brings us at once to religion, and to the shores of the vast uncharted seas of Mind whereon the orthodox religionist stands in pious fear of questing.

So great is this subject, and so vast the implications for all mankind, that one must tread warily and with reverence: observing the command to be as wise as a serpent but as harmless as a dove. For this reason I say to you that you would not understand all the things that have come to us through our investigations. Some of the things we have seen and heard you would not all credit, but you would

strain your imagination and might in consequence grow to be doubtful on the lesser
points. The day of full understanding, though
not far off, is not yet here, and it would be the
height of folly to risk the unveiling of too much.
Valuable minds, trembling upon the brink
between belief and no-belief, would either be
revolted or might even have their minds
unseated.

I declare to you that many things the world
has dubbed impossible are, in truth, quite possible. The amazing story of the New Testament: the so-called miracles, the marvellous
appearances, the Pentecostal miracle, the
mediumistic and occult phenomena, are all
true, or, at least, they are all possible. They
foreshadow a new life for the world: a life that
is as far above our present limited and semi-
animalic existence as the life of a plant is above
the life of the earth in which it grows. That
which was foreshadowed in the stories of the
Bible is now coming to full fruition in the world
—of that fact my researches convince me.

Read the New Testament again! Read it
in the light of what I have told you in these
chapters and you will find there a confirmation
of the reality of these new worlds into which
the human mind is just beginning to find entry
—and is, indeed, developing new faculties for
this glorious entry. You must not be despon-
dent if these faculties are not at present
developed in yourself: we are all parts of one

Mind and we each have our gifts, as Paul
rightly said. On the other hand, you should
not deny the existence of these psychic powers
in others just because you have never developed
them in yourself. If you want to realize how
very possible it is for there to be worlds about
you which you cannot sense, you should try to
imagine yourself living in a world where all but
a few men were blind, and where even the
few had only just begun to develop their
powers of vision. Would not those who were
blind find it difficult to believe the strange
stories told by those who could see? Since
vision has no meaning to a blind man, would
not all the meaning of Art and Colour, Design
and even Literature, be entirely lost upon this
imaginary blind world? Would not the Blind
Majority be utterly unable to understand what
the Seeing Minority had to tell them of their
marvellous New World, which, despite all its
newness, was really only a new aspect of the
Old World hitherto unperceived. Indeed this
is the case, and is doubly true now of the New
World being investigated by psychic science—
the New World which dawned upon humanity
through early Christianity, and which has been
waiting, in the stifling protection of the
churches, for the day of its full appearing—
when all men shall receive the "new sight" and
shall thus be able to make contact with a higher
plane of Life.

Religion in the main seems to have lost sight

of the meaning of this New World altogether. But through my investigations the old sayings of the Bible have been made to stand up and live in the colours of perfect Truth. Surely it is clear to all who read these pages that the promised "Coming of the Lord" is going to be the great day when all men shall be able to see the planes upon which all who have "passed over" are existing. When that day comes will not the same condemnation be made of our modern blind leaders of the blind as was made two thousand years ago when Jesus said: *Blind leaders of the blind . . . whited sepulchres . . . hypocrites . . . blind guides . . . proselytisers . . . vipers . . . You strain at a gnat and swallow a camel . . . You do all your works to be seen of men . . . You love the top seats at feasts. . . .*

What will that condemnation mean? No more nor less than that the churches, whilst struggling and contending over the gnats of sectarianism and dogma, are calmly swallowing the camel of ignorance in regard to the unseen Greater Worlds which exists all around us and about us. In my Father's house are many mansions, said Jesus of Nazareth. Indeed there are, and the doors of them all are open wide for those who seek.

One of the greatest testimonies I have ever received as to the real objective existence of this "New World," and one that has convinced me that all who have "eyes to see" can, and do, see the same things, has come quite recently from a man who has been conducting experiments (though he would not call them that) with these new faculties. The statements which he has sent me tally exactly with those I have set down here, and also with others which I feel it best to withhold as yet. These statements deal with the teachings of the Bible in regard to reincarnation and other matters. For example, it is stated by many hypnotic subjects who have sat for me that the claim that Christ was the son of David is based upon a literal interpretation and not merely upon fancy or symbolism. Listen to this message which has come to us from our friend, Mr. T., who has received it independently.

Even the Scribes and Pharisees could not answer the question: How is it possible for David to call Him both my Lord and my Son? The answer lies in the fact that Christ was a reincarnation of a son of David, now as the Messiah descended from the House of David, Jesus Christ is a reincarnation of Absalom who stole the hearts of Israel, and who was without spot or blemish. Who was He before He became the son of David? The son of God? He could be David, Lord and son by having lived past lives before being the son of David, and having been the Son of God in His first incarnation.

If this is so it lends weight to the idea of a Second Coming, which no longer may be interpreted merely as a symbol for the coming to power of an idea, nor just the enthronement of the Christian Faith. Such things may be

literal. In fact, that is my own interpretation:
I know Christ is coming again soon!

THE BOOK OF REVELATIONS

The objective nature of this unseen world
becomes startlingly obvious when we realize
the truth of the symbolism of Revelation.   Our
subjects often tell us things which explain and
confirm our suspicion that the Revelator wrote
His great vision in a trance, and that He, like
ourselves, was plumbing unknown depths of
the Universal Consciousness.   There is nothing
wrong or presumptuous or blasphemous in such
a statement; for we are all sons of God, and we
have all the right to seek for those "many
mansions" of which Jesus spoke, and to enter
therein.   We have developed the surface-
scratching of the Western psychologists along
lines indicated to us by the Great Ones of
Thibet, India and China, and in so doing we
have pierced the illusion of *Mayâ* (the Space-
Time aspect of this Universe) and have found
the reality there which the Revelator also
found.   In that reality the Future is as clear
as the Past, and the destiny of men, though
chosen by them in part, is written for all
to see.

This, indeed, the Revelator saw, and although
it may please the hardened materialist to call
his vision "an opium eater's dream," we know

that it was indeed nothing of the kind, and that John was in a state of trance-mediumship at the time of his vision. Do we not read: *I was in the spirit on the Lord's day** which, being interpreted, means, I was in a trance on the Lord's day.

It may be asked, What right have you to assume this interpretation? and my answer is, Turn to the fourth chapter of Revelation, and there in the first verse read how John heard a voice like a trumpet saying: *Come up hither, and I will show thee things which must be hereafter.*† Now those of us who are Fellows of the Royal Geographical Society will vouch for the fact that the isle of Patmos, where John was at the time, has no mountains. There is only one sound explanation of this command to come up hither, and that is the explanation that John was placed in a trance and made an astral journey. In fact, the sentence next after the command to go up reads as follows: *And immediately I was in the spirit.*‡ Allowing even for the errors of translation and the change in the meanings of words, the meaning of the passage is plain in the meaning of modern psychic science. It is possible that the Revelator's physical body actually wrote down the words of Revelation as his astral body heard the commands and witnessed the scenes in the astral world, for

---

* The Revelation 1 : 10. † The Revelation 4 : 1.
‡ The Revelation 4 : 2.

the astral body would be in complete telepathic communication with the physical
body,* just as an aeroplane keeps in touch
with its base by radio. The experiment with
thought-projection described earlier in these
pages confirms the truth of this telepathic
connection.

Astral journeys are now a well-attested fact,
and they explain many of the things in the Bible
which have hitherto been obscure to many
people. In Revelation, chapter xxi, verse 10,
we read: *And he carried me away in the spirit to a
great and high mountain.* This obviously refers to
astral journeying. It is also quite an established
fact that dreams are often connected with
astral journeys. The sights seen are real sights,
and the sounds heard are real sounds. I know
of a man, an experimenter with psychic matters, whose subject once awakened him in the
early morning and, standing patiently at the
foot of his bed, complained that she could not
sleep. "*Go back to bed, and go to sleep,*" commanded the man, "*and do not awaken until nine
o'clock.*" THE GIRL WENT STRAIGHT BACK TO
HER BED NINETY MILES AWAY AND SLEPT SOUNDLY
UNTIL NINE O'CLOCK. Was this not an astral
journey made by this girl to the bedside of her
master? You say, No, the man had a dream.
To which I make reply, The girl knew she was
going to see him and ask to be sent to sleep,

* See THE INVISIBLE INFLUENCE, pp. 56, 57, 58, 59, 60, 61 for
demonstrations with subjects.

and she was quite conscious of awakening him and of standing by his bedside. This event took place but a few years ago and I know both people well, as does also my publisher and many others. He is just a very humble and kindly man, and the girl charming, also, but they are both of the sort that the churches have rejected in their insistence upon temporal power.

Much as "pillars of the church" would be horrified to know it, I declare that the early Christian community was built upon this power. What were the disciples before the resurrection? Until that demonstration of the conquest of death, and the testimony which it provided, they were a very poor lot of men, without enough courage to stand by their Master. The Christian world was built upon a knowledge of the psychic world, and only upon such knowledge can it endure.

Have we not read that both Peter and Paul have said in the Bible, *I was in a trance.** What else could this mean except that they were in a mediumistic state? Paul says quite plainly to one of the churches: *I thank my God, I speak with tongues more than ye all: yet in the Church I had rather speak five words with my understanding.*† This can only imply that he preached most of his sermons in the trance state and could not control his words or remember them after-

---

* Acts 10 : 10. . . . he (Peter) fell into a trance.
† 1 Corinthians 14 : 18-19.

wards. There is no other meaning possible. I strongly recommend all great thinkers to read Corinthians, and Ephesians, which are the writings of Paul the Saint, and above all do I counsel them to study the great Book of Revelation.

For in Revelation is the key to much of our modern dilemma. Even the great plagues that were foretold in Revelation are beginning to manifest in the world. Have we not a plague of tuberculosis, and a plague of cancer, and a plague of battle-planes which, like the scorpions of the Revelator, will become a devastating force when Armageddon breaks in the near future.

The dis-ease* plagues are of special interest to all medical men, as well as to a great section of the public, and the two modern plagues, cancer and tuberculosis, may be briefly reviewed here. Tuberculosis has definitely been shown to have a "causal" micro-organism, the tubercle bacillus, whilst cancer has not. The fact has, however, been completely overlooked that these micro-organisms are not the cause of the dis-ease at all, but its immediate result. Micro-organisms are protein bodies electrically formed by the human body to act

---

*Notice that I have throughout spelled the word "disease" as DIS-EASE. This is not a mere fad, but the idea is to impress upon your unconsciousness the tremendous fact that disease is not just something mechanical but that it is DIS-EASE—a mind-body not at ease. This is the basis of the New Testament miracles of healing.

as protectors against the ravages of the dis-ease. The more powerful the attack of the dis-ease the greater will be the number of micro-organisms, or germs, formed. This fact, which seemed to be an added reason in support of the germ-theory, explains why it is that germs (so-called), when injected into the body, will produce the dis-ease. The real reason is that they produce those electrical (a low level of the mental) conditions in the body which constitute the dis-ease. This also explains why a vaccine is at times so successful in curing dis-ease. When the protein "germ"-cell is injected into a human body in a dead, or partially dead, state, it has the effect, though too impotent to produce the dis-ease, of stimulating the growth of extra-resistance-tissue which in turn produces electrical conditions inimical to the continuance of the particular dis-ease-vibration in the body. To understand this fact completely you must understand that all dis-ease is a vibratory disorder.

There is another very good reason why this interpretation of the nature of the protein (mis-called germ) is perfectly logical and why it satisfies medical science in the light of Kock's postulates. For when not affected by heat, this protein will attract the electrical charge which constitutes the dis-ease and for this reason it is that the body produces them. They are not the invaders, these so-called germs, but they are the protectors of the body. In performing their task great electrical and incidentally thermal energy is released, and this is frequently recorded as a high-temperature in the patient. This temperature tends to render the protein impotent, for even crystals are killed by heat, and the same applies to the protein. This "killing" really means that, both in the crystals and in the protein, the vibratory period is changed or stopped.

Let me repeat a great Truth: BACTERIA ARE NOT THE CAUSE OF DIS-EASE BUT THE IMMEDIATE RESULT OF A DISORDERED VIBRATION TERMED DIS-EASE. *This truth was communicated to me one night recently by the great White Lodge of Thibet.* It is a knowledge which the West has despised for years in its arrogant assumption of the intellect. But it is part of the knowledge which humanity must learn, and when it begins to study dis-ease in this new light, a great disease-less future will dawn for the world. Remember this is where medicine links up with religion: this is where the science of medicine becomes a science of the mind-power of the human body, and where medicine takes its place in the grand scheme of knowledge which constitutes the Science of the Kingdom. Once men begin to think along these lines discoveries will begin to open up on every side, and the rush of evidence will be overwhelming.

We must all face the facts and realize that "wireless apparatuses" like the Abrahams' box,* and the Richards' diagnostic set†, are by no means all humbug and eye-wash. Once it is realized that dis-ease is a vibratory disorder, electrical apparatus for detecting its presence and curing its ravages becomes an obvious desiderata. Therefore, in the light of this great truth, these "wireless dis-ease detectors" ought, at least, to be investigated with an open mind. I would let the honest seeker after Truth test all things, secure in the knowledge that, so long as he were honest, he would be bound to be safely guided, and that if he were not honest then he would simply use the rope given him to hang himself.

We have still to be humble and to be willing to learn the great Truths which Pythagoras taught *circa* B.C. 562. For he taught that everything that exists is a vibration, and the more we know of the Universe the more we realize this to be true.

The physical electrical apparatus devised by advanced Western thinkers as dis-ease detectors are, however, but faint foreshadows of the great

---

* Abrahams' box was an invention by Doctor Abrahams of California, U.S.A. It was an electrical apparatus so designed that a sick person could be attached to it and thereby connected electrically to a perfectly healthy subject. The diagnosis was made by the reaction of the subject to this connection. In the light of my statements the reader will discern a very distinct likeness between the physical contact obtained through the Abrahams' box, and the psychic contact obtained by the use of a trance-medium.

† Dr. Richards is a medical colleague. He has shown that the atomic weights of various compounds coincide with their vibratory periods, and that any activity or change of activity in a human organ can be interpreted and recorded in terms of vibration.

fact manifested by the trance-medium when he diagnoses dis-ease by registering the vibrations coming from a human body. Also it can be understood why mental and spiritual healing is not different from healing by drugs in its kind, but in its degree. The healing by drugs is a clumsy way of restoring the electrical balance of the.body, and could be much more directly carried out by the mind, for the mind, in its instinctive state, acting through its instinctive mind-centres, controls the electrical vibrations of the body. This will explain why it is that the production of the "psychic state" in a patient, either by hypnotism, or by the use of a trance-medium, or by the giving of certain drugs (which really act on the sympathetic plexuses in the bowels), or by electrical stimulus, can all cure dis-ease.

Incidentally, the fact that the health or ill-health of the body is vibratory and magnetic, should warn people that the wearing of composition soles and heels on their shoes is likely to have an adverse effect upon their health. The human mind-body is supplied with energy from the Earth no less than is the plant: but whereas the plant takes its energy through its roots, man takes his energy through his body in the form of magnetism from the Earth-currents. Rubber foot-wear of all sorts, by cutting man off from the magnetic Earth contact, is responsible for many of the functional nervous diseases of to-day.

Faith, if it is strong enough, can also cure dis-ease, for strong faith will cause the vibratory period to be changed to its normal rate. All this wisdom hinges on a knowledge of the existence of the astral body, and a knowledge of the way in which the physical body is affected by the astral. In the case of faith-healing, an even further plane of energy is brought into play, for faith-healing comes about through the control of the astral body by the perfect etheric body, and the resultant effect upon the physical.

All things in this world, including the body and its health and dis-ease, resolve at a final analysis into vibrations, and the larger cycles in which the vibrations are manifested. The social body, no less than the physical body, manifests this same *periodicity*, for the record of booms and slumps, peace and war, shows a remarkable periodicity.

The periodicity of recurring dis-ease (and war is most decidedly a social dis-ease in the social body) is the basis of an interesting prophecy worked out by my literary friend Mr. Stanley de Brath, Scholar, and Editor of PSYCHIC SCIENCE. In the issue of that journal for July, 1934 (Vol. XIII, No. 2), which every-one should read, Mr. de Brath makes the following computation to show that Armageddon is due in 1937.

1857, Indian Mutiny which lasted one year=1858.

1858—to this add 1858 as follows :

1
8
5
8
———
1880
———

1880, Egyptian War which lasted one year=1881.

1881—to this add 1881 as follows :

1
8
8
1
———
1899
———

1899, Boer War which lasted three years=1902.

1902—to this add 1902 as follows:

1
9
0
2
———
1914
———

1914, Great War which lasted four years=1918.

$$
\begin{array}{r}
1918 \\
1 \\
9 \\
1 \\
8 \\
\hline
1937 \\
\hline
\end{array}
$$

The powers of prophecy are not, therefore, based upon irrational premises. In the Science of the Kingdom there is plenty of room for prophecy as a rational and natural extension of man's at present limited powers. That is why the record of the Bible is so important. It is the great record of the New Science.

I have referred frequently in these writings to the Holy Bible, and I want once again to impress upon my readers the necessity for getting out of their minds any remaining feelings that it is a sentimental book. For our psychic research has shown us beyond dispute that the Bible is the great Text Book of the New Science which is rapidly replacing the science of the old world that is doomed to end soon. The Bible is a text book and a guide to the Science of the Kingdom of God.

All who have eyes to see may read and observe the contact points which have of late been made between the old scientists and the

New Science. How clearly, for example, is the spiritual law of the Bible confirmed in the latest admissions of the great mathematicians and astronomers. Sir James Jeans said in his book THIS MYSTERIOUS UNIVERSE that the Universe was like the thinking of a great mathematician. Does not the Bible make this fact as clear as day? All the symbolism of the Bible shows the tremendous importance of numbers. There is a reason why all the great symbols and movements are numbered in sevens: seven Angels, seven Spirits, seven Stars, seven Trumpets, seven Days of Creation, and many others are all found throughout the Bible and especially in Revelation. This indicates that the Universe is based upon a reality which even mathematics, though it shows the nature of this reality in terms of numbers, can never explain. *The sevenfold nature of phenomena is everywhere observable*, for phenomena but obey the unseen laws of the invisible Kingdom. Thus we find that there are seven notes of music, seven colours in the visible spectrum, and even seven main atomic groups. The seventh wave is alleged to be the largest of its series because of the fact that it gathers up the backwash of the previous six waves. There are even seven heavens, or seven mental states of progression.

There are *seven* colours, each representing the *seven* great realities of the Universe of Life: Violet=*understanding;* Indigo=*wisdom;* Blue=*life;* Green=*modesty;* yellow=*honesty;* Orange=

love; Red=*truth.* The meaning of modesty here is SIMPLICITY, the key-note to the teachings of Jesus: *Unless ye become as a little child, ye cannot enter the Kingdom of Heaven.* What does a child do? He asks questions. He wants to know. Do *you* seek to understand?

These great *seven* colours each have attached to it one of the *seven* notes of music, and one of the *seven* primary perfumes or scents. The hypnotic trance subject sees clearly these colours and is aware of these perfumes as the different notes are played, hence the origin of *Colour-music* (*seven* colours to *seven* notes), and what will become the greatest of all music, the *Perfume-colour-music* which simulates the Heavenly Music. (In this direction we must not forget also the *seven* continents, the *seven* seas, and the *seven* planets, apart from other references to this perfect number seven).

If the colours are not blended they are said to be *simple* colours; all great teachers are said to talk in *simple* language; *seven* is the Heavenly perfection expressed in *simple* numbers. Christ taught only one thing whilst on Earth but it meant everything to those who live on Earth: SIMPLICITY is the key to the entry into *the Kingdom of Heaven* (HAPPINESS) which *is within you.* Don't make a mystery of anything: whenever there is a simple explanation of anything do not look for a complex statement. SIMPLICITY IS THE SECRET OF LIFE, THE FOUNDATION OF HAPPINESS, AND THE ESSENCE OF GOD.

The great Eastern teaching is that man has
seven mind-centres (called *Chakras*) and this
fact can be readily proven to those willing to
learn. This great teaching explains many
things which Western medicine cannot explain,
among which are certain phenomena resulting
from head-injuries, shell-shock, and hysteria—
about all of which we learned more during the
last war than we should learn in generations of
peace. These seven mind-centres are not con-
fined to the brain, anatomically speaking, but
they are distributed over the trunk. In fact,
the solar-plexus is composed of grey matter
(nerve cells and ganglia) just as is the brain,
and is part of the physical antenna for receiving
the telepathic messages of the instinctive mind.

The Eastern adepts know far more about the
mind than do our psychologists, and also more
about the body-mind mechanism than do our
anatomists. For instance, the pineal gland,
which is the most important endocrine gland
in the body, has been known to the East for
ages as one of the vital mind-centres of the
body, but has been called "brain-sand" by the
physiologists and anatomists of the West, and
relegated to the dust-heap.

Almost overpowering witness to the potency
of the *chakras* or mind-centres is given by the
fact that all genuine cases of mental deficiency,
and the majority of cases of mental disorder,
are suffering from irregular placement of
the vertebræ. These misplacements of the

vertebræ press upon the mind-centres of the human trunk (the *chakras*) and are the cause of the mental state. Once the body is looked upon as a receiver of telepathic power, then all its ills become naturally due to non-reception, mis-tuning, or a defect in the receiving-apparatus. In other words, the body is seen to have no power of itself to become ill, but is ill only as a result of being untuned or mis-tuned to the telepathic waves of mental power which constitute Life.

If misplaced vertebræ are corrected early in life, their owner will become almost normal—the degree of normality depending upon how soon after birth the defect of the spine was corrected. In later life it is not only the endocrine glands, etc., which are responsible for insanity, but also those alterations in the vertebral column which occur with such diseases as hyptonia of muscles, "ossification" of one vertebra to another, and the effect which obesity has of causing the abdominal muscles to pull on the solar plexus and the other mind-centres of the trunk. These are urgent matters for investigation by the Board of Control in Lunacy.

Francis J. Mott in his LAW EMERGES * made some very interesting comments upon the sevenfold nature of the universe. His book, dealing with the discovery of a universal design of Life by a Mrs. Bill, sets out the following data:

---

* Temporarily out of print. To be re-issued shortly under the title of HARNESSING LIFE.

It is well-known that the decimal expressions of the seven parts of unity are as follows:

One-seventh	=	0.142857˙
Two-sevenths	=	0.285714˙
Three-sevenths	=	0.428571˙
Four-sevenths	=	0.571428˙
Five-sevenths	=	0.714285˙
Six-sevenths	=	0.857142˙

the whole of the six figures being recurring.

I ask my reader particularly to note that the same numbers recur in the same order throughout, and that each decimal is recurring at the sixth digit. Now, there is a way in which the whole of the above expressions can be set out satisfactorily: this is in the form of a wheel, as follows:

Observe, that no matter at which point one starts to follow the expression, the completion thereof is a matter, not of seconds, not of years, nor even of æons, but of eternity. You have here a perfect mathematical symbol of perpetual motion, or infinite progression, always drawing nearer to unity but never achieving its expression.

The mathematician and the scientist have

almost given up trying to explain the Universe, and where they are still trying their writings sound more like sermons than scientific treatises. No wonder, for the days of the outpouring of the Spirit have arrived. How near these days are you must not know, except you have ears to hear and eyes to see. Through the mouths of many hypnotic subjects the warning is continually being received by us that the end of the world is upon us. Prophecy which it would be dangerous, or at least unwise, to publish now—but written evidence of which is in the hands of reputable witnesses for confirmation when the time arrives—makes it clear to me that sweeping international and political changes may be expected during the next few months. Cabinet positions will change in this country, and the leading positions of the State of England will undergo vital changes. That is the substance of the prophecies which come through the mouths of our trance subjects, and with one accord they indicate that the time is ripe for these changes, and that when they occur the Day of the Lord, as it is called, will be close at hand.

In that time, which is coming fast upon us, neither Communist, nor Fascist, Socialist nor Tory will be of importance to the world, for there will be nothing but a common humanity with a waiting face uplifted to see the Glory of the Lord.

And so I come to the close of my revelation

to you of great truths which can never die and of wonders which you will yet see.

In this world of chaos and darkness you have a work which no other can do and to neglect it is one of the greatest crimes a soul can commit now and throughout Eternity.

Webster rightly stated: *There is nothing so powerful as truth, yet often nothing so strange.*

In this book there are secrets which are worth their weight in gold: I humbly submit that, although all it contains are facts, it was through inspiration given to me by my Masters in the Himalayas and the Greater World (as yet invisible to many) that it became possible to make known to the world the facts contained in this work. And now *I commend my philosophy to you*, knowing that it will lead you to power, to prosperity, to happiness, to love and to the life-everlasting; showing you the way to the Great Fountain and Giver of all life, God Himself—so long as you obey His law. I therefore close this chapter with the telling command:

Dare to do right; dare to be true:
*   You have a work which no other can do.*
Do it so bravely, so kindly, so well;
*   Angels will hasten the story to tell !*

Dare to do right; dare to be true:
*   Other men's failures can never save you.*
Stand by your conscience, your honour, your faith;
*   Stand like a hero and battle till death* (so called).

Dare to do right; dare to be true;
  Jesus, your Saviour, will carry you through,
City, and Mansion, and Throne all in sight;
  Can you not dare to be true and do right?